Looking At Sociology, and Education: A New Perspective

Mutubuki Edias Henry

Table of Contents

Foreword

It gives me great pleasure to write a foreword to this vital publication. It covers a wide and deep spectrum of sociological cum educational issues. It is a classic of sociological and educational exposition. One would expect no less of a book from a master of sociology and an expert on education.

What particularly impress me are several new perspectives on sociological issues. The author introduces, hitherto unknown founder makers of sociology, namely Akhenaton and Khaldun, both persons of African descent. It is placing sociology in the African context, and flavor. Secondly, the author proffers interesting socio cultural conveyance systems, namely enculturation, diffusion, osmosis and rhizomery. These greatly help to explain variations in socio culture among social groups in the world. Thirdly, on controversy in religion, he brings out social facts relating to religion, in particular the fact that more than half of the world population do not believe in God, or supernatural power. Yet they prosper and progress better than the supernatural fearing people. They seem to be more compassionate and generous than their God fearing counterparts.

On methods of studying sociology, the author successfully blends research paradigms, methods, instruments with their essential tools descriptive statistics, information technology and referencing conventions. On sociological theories and education I find a refreshing application of macro, micro and radical perspectives to education. An essential chapter on Education, Justice and Social Values spans the links between education, justice, universal human rights and social norms. Social justice and human rights education is critical to peace and harmony in the world.

The book ends appropriately with a chapter on great figures in sociology. Here the author presents a figure, summarizes his ideas, then artistically weaves in analyses and applications relevant to the African social conditions. To cap it all, a comprehensive glossary covers basic terms very well. It is a stand-alone quick referencing section.

I would like to conclude by strongly recommending all students and staff to read and study the many useful aspects covered in this great book.

Professor Gwirayi Pesanayi
Great Zimbabwe University

Preface

The aim of this book is the understanding and appreciation of sociology, and sociology of education. It is about the theory and practice of sociology, not a treatise in sociology. Thus, its perspective is broader, eclectic and more general than that of a textbook on sociology. It is intended to be an introduction to other literature of sociology. Because no one work could cover all the literature in this field, my intent was to select the theory and practice that is most relevant and useful in understanding and analyzing behaviour, action and activities in society. The selection also takes into account those practices, processes and problems that are commonly met by students in tertiary institutions, in particular, at the undergraduate, graduate and post graduate levels. It is hoped this audience finds in this book useful applicable methods of description and analysis of social and contemporary issues. It is specially designed as a sensitizing, teaching and learning vehicle. Thus, it is a source book on the many dimensions of sociology as a discipline. Social phenomena and reality, being of diverse nature, cannot be grasped except through a multi dimensional approach in which concepts and ideas prove useful at different stages of development. This is especially true of the contemporary world which is witnessing rapid and comprehensive processes of social transformation.

I hope to convey a sense of the significance of sociology both as a human activity and as an intellectual discipline. It is also intended to introduce important concepts involved in the study of sociology. The book tries to establish the interrelations of sociology as a process with other social processes. There is great need today in the field of sociology, and sociology of education, for adequate, relevant and user friendly books whose conceptual tools can realistically and significantly describe concepts and processes which must provide the basis for effective observation and analysis.

Included in the book are relevant topics on figures and statistics in sociology and education. There is a relevant section on information, technology and communication as they relate to sociological studies. All these are relevant and topical to the student, and reader. Included at the end is a comprehensive, instructing and elaborate glossary of terms used, and implied, in the book. The glossary, in itself, is intended to act as a quick reference teaching and learning unit. Technical or new terms in the book are also explained within the text. Possible questions for reflection are included towards the end of a chapter. The over all intention is to make this book, a one stop, one shop text for the student of sociology.

In writing this book I owe debts of gratitude to many people and institutions. First, to the generations of my teachers who initiated me into the academic world. Secondly, there are the generations of students to whom I have taught courses on theory and applied sociology. They have therefore, been some form of guinea pigs for many of the ideas expressed in this book. Thirdly, there are many of my colleagues who have inspired me to immortalize my many years of teaching experiences into a book. It is tempting to name them, but that can create problems except if it is possible to name all. All the same I am indebted to all who have assisted in various ways in the preparation and publication of this book.

In a special category stands my life partner, Laura MazilaNkata Tshambiwa waMashu, who has been my constant companion and a source of inspiration throughout my academic and professional odyssey.

Preface to the Canadian Edition

I wish to express my profound gratitude to many readers' very useful suggestions. I have endeavoured to include the interesting, constructive and well meaning suggestions in the Canadian edition. It is also gratifying to note that the Canadian edition has come so soon.

I have made some additions and alterations to the first edition. By popular request I have added a lengthy section on justice, universal human rights and the International Court of Justice. There is a burning need for learning, teaching and understanding of these critical areas for peace and harmony to prevail in the world. There is also an important section on deviance, discipline and social control. Most of the world's social problems emanate from social, political, economic and religious deviance. There is a lot of deviance in the world by the young and old, leaders and led, rich and poor, powerful and weak, priest and laity.

I have also expanded on Max Weber's power and authority to include administration, management and their attendant variations. I have also provided more alternative reading, tasks and fresh emphases, seldom to introducing additions and corrections. I hope the book continues to challenge and stimulate you, the reader, to wonder about social things you might otherwise have ignored.

E.H. Mutubuki
Faculty of Education
Midlands State University

Chapter 1: Why Sociology?

We all live in a world with, and of, others. No person is an island. It is almost impossible to live a life of a hermit. A new born baby cannot do without another human being. It will not be able to survive without the intervention of another human being. Even the celebrated stories of children having been brought up by animals, such as wolves, also underline the need for some adult creature to take care of the very young ones. In other words the young need to be fed, clothed, taught a language. They need to interact with others, learn social values and so on. All this is the process of socialization.

So it is imperative that we have a good, sound and better understanding of how people are born, and bred; how they live, develop, grow up and eventually die. So sociology is interested in the study of humankind, of past and present people and their ways of living. But sociologists never base their general theoretical and practical findings on the study of a single group, population, race, tribe, class, nation, time, or place. Now more than ever before, people from different parts of the world who speak different languages, who possess different social backgrounds, values and beliefs find themselves closer together in a new global village. To all these members of the global community sociology offers an indispensable opportunity to examine, explain, and enjoy human diversity. All people and socio-cultures are equally worthy of study. Sociology would teach us that, in spite of our human differences, the difference is the same. We are all members of the same family, of the same species. Most likely, sociology has much to contribute to the understanding of the major issues that divide, and should unite, contemporary society and endanger, or promote world peace.

In other words, sociology contributes to social study and criticism. It helps to expand the boundaries of human compassion, and commitment to action. It can lead to an understanding of given sets of social situations and circumstances. It can provide means of increasing socio-cultural sensitivity, permitting policies to be based on diversities in cultural values. And perhaps, more significant, it makes individuals and groups aware of their own place in the social schemes of their lives. Sociologically speaking, all individuals should have the right to their point of view, the right to develop to the full limits of their capacities, as long as this does not impinge on the rights of others.

Sociology is a form of consciousness and an attempt to understand what is unique about human beings. Sociology continually emphasizes the relativity of ideas, truth, and reality itself. Sociology teaches us that things are not what they seem. Social reality turns out to have many layers of meaning. The discovery of each new layer changes the perception of the whole (Berger, 1967). Reality is something determined by social consensus. People may refuse to accept what could be real. A good example is the African story of the one eyed person in the land of the blind. The one eyed person came to the land and began to tell as well as describe how things really were. The person described the blue sky, the white clouds, the trees that were green with beautiful colours on them. But the blind people would not believe the one eyed person, so they blinded his good eye. Then the person too, perceived things as they originally were to the land of the blind. What is real differs from place to place as well as from time to time. People in different socio-cultures perceive similar things and events from entirely different perspectives, and they react differently.

What is Sociology?

Essentially sociology is concerned with understanding the nature of the social world. Sociology is also a way of thinking about the social world. It is seen as a way of describing and explaining the activities of the socio-cultural world so as to develop an understanding of human social organization and behaviour. However, there are many different ways of looking at, and interpreting the actions of others and thus of analyzing and explaining the social world. We call these different ways of looking at the social world sociological perspectives. Each viewpoint, or perspective, or orientation is based on different starting assumptions about how the social world is established and maintained. How individuals and groups operate within the given socio-cultural world can be viewed from different viewpoints. There seems to be no correct or wrong orientation. The many varied orientations tend to confuse the beginning student of sociology since each viewpoint leads to a different picture of the social world. It is important to note that each viewpoint helps to explain social phenomena that can also be explained from a different perspective. These are fascinating challenges that sociology brings to the learning arena.

Sociology can be defined as a systematic study of human societies through out the ages, that is, the past, present and the future. So its primary purpose is the attempt to understand the far-reaching changes that occur in human societies. Society is more than a collection of individuals staying together, with a shared way of life. Society is a definite, determinate network of associations, institutions, groups with socio cultural symbols and values interwoven among them. All these help to bind them as a social group. Major and minor social shifts that occur in people's lives are of interest to the student of sociology. Sociological research aims to distinguish between intended and unintended results of human action. The resulting balance between social reproduction and social transformation should be studied. Social reproduction refers to the way societies keep going, maintaining the same social patterns and processes. Social transformation refers to the changes societies undergo. Sociology also involves the ability to think imaginatively and to detach oneself from bias and preconceived ideas about social events and processes.

This is also referred to as sociological imagination. It is a way of examining the varied relations among people as they seek answers to questions that puzzle them about people and society. Some of these questions are concerned with what all people and their societies have in common through out time. In sociology we say these questions and issues are of a trans-historical nature. But there are those that arise out of people's experiences living in particular historical epochs and types of society. We refer to these as being historically specific. Even contemporary social problems and phenomena have their roots in historically specific conceptions. Examples are capitalism, socialism, bureaucracy, mass society, class, race and gender.

In short, sociology is a science in that it involves systematic methods of investigation and the assessment and evaluation of theories in the light of evidence and logical argument. It should not, however, be confused with the methods of the natural sciences, because studying human behaviour is basically different from studying fauna and flora.

Some of the most eminent founders of sociology are Akhenaton Amenotope, Khaldun Ibn, Auguste Comte, Emile Durkheim, Karl Marx, and Max Weber who wrote extensively concerning the nature of sociology and its impact on the development of the social world. They endeavoured to ask and answer questions like: What is nature? What are people? Why is society made up as it is? Why and how do societies change?

Auguste Comte (1798-1857) is said to have invented the term sociology. Before then he had used the term social physics which he found in conflict with other people's areas of study. He saw sociology as the natural branch of science to follow physics, chemistry and biology. He saw sociology contributing greatly to the welfare of humanity. It was the jewel in the crown of human social understanding. He later on drew up ambitious plans for the reconstruction of French society, and for humanity too.

Some Broad Concepts that are used in this Book

Sociology, like any other discipline, operates on certain basic concepts, definitions and settings. These basic concepts are lenses through which a sociologist looks at social reality. They are the building blocks with which the sociologist constructs historically specific social phenomena. Even contemporary issues are examined through the use of these basic concepts.

Sociology is a coined word from two concepts, socio: of life between people, human interaction, inter-relationship; and ology, the study of whatever area. The term is derived from the Latin word *socitus* meaning society and logos, a Greek word meaning knowledge. So sociology can be viewed as the systematic study of a human being relating with one or more human beings; the study of groups in society and their institutions, their practices, beliefs, values, norms…in short their socio-culture. We will visit this concept more as we go on with our study.

It is important to explain what we mean by humans. The term human comes from a zoological term homonoid. Homonoids consist of primates such as apes, chimpanzees, monkeys, gorillas, baboons, and us humans. We share a lot of genetic and social characteristics: Hence they are our biological cousins. We call ourselves homo(noid) sapiens, sapiens is Latin meaning intelligent. Whether we are intelligent is a source of debate amongst social scientists given our actions, products and processes on earth. There are basic elements of humans. These include biological map consisting genes, chromosomes and physical features. The chromosomes give rise to sex characteristics female and male. These give rise to social gender attributes with varied status and roles.

Because we are gregarious we tend to live in groups for safety, security and unity of purpose in solving problems of existence, we develop elements of social characteristics. As humans we have four basic social characteristics. First, we have identity markers such as names, group, area of origin, totems, language. Second, humans have socio culture, a way of life consisting of norms, mores and values. We come back to this aspect later in the chapter. Third, humans exhibit artifacts in their daily lives such as shelter, clothes, tools, utensils, weapons, and technology. Four, humans have language shared by the group. Language can be verbal, oral, written, and non verbal with symbols, gestures, grunts and slogans.

Culture and society: In order to survive and develop a new born baby has to learn the skills, knowledge and accepted ways of behaving of the people (society) into which it is born. In sociological terms, it must learn the culture of its society. Culture is the way of life of a social group as manifested in the patterns of behaviour of its members and in relation to all the material and non-material products of group life that people acquire as members of society. Linton (1984) states that the culture of a society is the way of life of its members; the collection of ideas and habits which they learn, share and transmit from generation to generation. So culture is a design for living, cherished by members of a particular society. Culture has two essential elements, first, it is learned; second, it is shared. Without a shared culture, members of society would be unable to cooperate and communicate. Confusion and disorder would ensue. The material and socio cultural circumstances of the family into which an individual is born will have an enormous determining influence on his/her life chances.

Culture and behaviour: Culture determines, to a very large extent, how members think, feel and act. Culture directs action, feelings and hence behaviour. It defines their outlook on life. It defines accepted ways of behaving. Such definitions vary from society to society.

Socialization stands for the whole range of learning situations, starting at birth and continuing into old age. So socialization is a process through which the culture of a society is transmitted to its new and uninitiated members. It is a process whereby the individual becomes a person (Ogburn, 1982). Primary socialization takes place during infancy, usually within the family. Secondary socialization takes place through agencies like the education system, occupational groups, peer groups. Tertiary socialization involves adult social activities such as recreational associations, religious groupings, anniversary clubs and occupational associations. Without socialization, an individual would bear little resemblance to any human being defined as such.

Norms are standards of behaviour shared by members of a social group. Every culture has a number of guidelines that direct conduct in particular situations. So a norm is a specific guide to action which defines acceptable and appropriate behaviour in given situations, for example dress (male/female, for a dance, dinner, funeral, swim, building site). Norms are enforced by positive and negative sanctions, that is, rewards and punishments. Rewards and punishment are used to encourage or discourage certain types of behaviour. Examples of positive sanctions are applause, praise, and material rewards. Negative sanctions range from a look of disapproval to the death sentence. Sanctions can be formal or informal. So, norms are a major part of mechanisms of social control which help maintain order in society (Datta, 1986). Norms are classified according to the degree of severity, specificity, and certainty of sanctions imposed if they are violated. Examples of norms are laws, constitutions, rules and regulations, religious commandments, vows, and contracts. These are enforced by specially designated officials, or agencies, such as judges, prosecutors, police, courts and juries.

Mores are norms which, when violated, evoke a reaction of intense indignation and moral outrage leading to severe sanctions. They are social conventions considered essential to a group or community. Social mores are characterized by strong moral meaning and conformity to them is obligatory in a group or society. Examples of mores are the incest taboo, rape especially of minor children and the disabled, the prohibition of adultery, infanticide and geronticide.

Values concern general ideas of the desirable which guide choices of material objects and behaviour. Unlike norms values provide more general guidelines. A value is a belief that something is good and desirable. It defines what is important, worthwhile and worth striving for. Examples are justice, fairness, equality, patriotism, value of materialism, individual achievement, and postponement of gratification. Custom and fashion are values that when violated evoke ridicule or ostracism

Status: All members of society occupy a number of social positions known as statuses. A status is a position in society or group defined in terms of specific rights and obligations pertaining to the position. Examples of statuses are: *occupational* status such as teacher, doctor, lawyer, bus driver; *family* status: daughter, son, father, mother;

gender status: male, female; *racial* status: African, European, Asian, Coloured. Statuses are culturally defined, in spite of the fact that they may be based on biological factors such as sex or race. Some statuses are relatively fixed as individuals may not change their assignment to particular social positions. Examples of fixed or ascribed statuses are gender, race or aristocratic titles. Aristocratic titles, though, might change through revolutions or social upheavals.

Statuses that are not fixed, by biological characteristics, inheritance, or other factors over which individuals have no control, are called achieved statuses. Achieved status is a result of some degree of purposive action and choice. Examples are marital status, occupational status. At times the difference between achieved and ascribed statuses is not as clear-cut.

Role is expected behaviour corresponding to a social position. Each position in society is accompanied by a number of norms and values that define how an individual occupying a given status is expected to act. We can compare the role of husband or father, wife or mother, doctor or parent. So playing or performing roles involves social relationships in relation to other roles: doctor/patient, teacher/pupil, husband/wife and so on. Social roles regulate and organize behaviour. They provide means for accomplishing certain tasks.

Appropriate roles involve the exclusion of other areas of life in order to concentrate on the matter at hand. Roles provide social life with order and predictability. Interacting in terms of their respective roles people know what, when and how to do it. With the knowledge of each other's roles, each one is able to predict and comprehend the actions of the other. As an aspect of culture, roles provide an important part of the guidelines and directives necessary for an ordered society.

We have general sociological terms which a student of sociology should be familiar with. There are a number of them.

The term *institution* is used by sociologists to refer to basic focuses of social organization, which are common to all societies, dealing with basic universal challenges of ordered social life. Institutions involve regulated patterns of behaviour of individuals in society according to some definite norms and values. The home world, and the everyday life revolve on institutions such as the family, marriage, kinship, work, religion. Everyday life takes place within the context of established institutional order.

Education is a term that is derived from the Latin word *educare* which means to nurture, to care wholly. The human child is born helpless, culture-less, language-less. It has to acquire, that is to learn, all the language, survival skills, values, norms, patterns of behaviour, skills, wisdom etc of its group. As the child grows up it moves through the informal, formal and non-formal learning education systems and processes.

It is one thing to be schooled, learned, but another thing to be educated. There must be as many different definitions of education as there are schools of thought, each with its own particular sociological, philosophical, cultural, political, ideological, psychological or spiritual perspective. But education can safely be defined, or rather thought of, as

> *those processes of learning which enable a person to acquire all the skills (3Rs),*
> *behaviours, knowledge, values and norms which are considered worthwhile in*
> *the society to which one belongs…and as a person adapts to the environment*

In other words, being educated implies civilized behaviour, academic accomplishment, possession of a sound, reliable and upright character, maturity and responsibility. One should also be well versed in the traditions and ways of life of the people, be tolerant and accommodating, be open to other points of view; should spend time and resources profitably and wisely.

Sociology and Education are linked in many ways. Sociology and education have long roots. Sociological theories, methods and findings can be of service to education, just as they can be of service to science, literature, history, medicine, theology. What, when, why and how to teach or learn is based on fundamental philosophic, psychological and sociological principles. So the close relationship between sociology and education cannot be of service unless the nature of sociology and its limitations are understood first. But sociology and education suggest that there are two separate components or disciplines which are desperately trying to link together.

Sociology of Education places education in the centre, with sociology becoming the tool with which to examine the subject matter, namely education. Sociology of (medicine, religion, education etc) implies an inquiry into the nature of the field in question. Sociology of education provides a thorough and hard look at the educational system, its practices, processes and products. It provides an analysis and deep reflection in an effort to produce an effective, better alternative system. So sociology of education means the process of analysis, and reflection, and the product of that reflection. So sociology of education is the application of sociology to education.

Sociological Foundations of Education deal with the thoughts, researches, experiences and opinions of great thinkers in different eras focusing our attention on educational issues and universal questions. It is almost unthinkable to learn sociology of education without the great names, the gurus, like Akhenaton, Auguste Comte, Emile Durkheim, Karl Marx, Max Weber, Bronislaw Malinowisky, Jomo Kenyatta, Julius Kambarage Nyerere, to name a few. The geographical setting, and the time setting, of a thinker have a lot to do with the social values of the people, their culture, socialization and education. Sociology here makes reference to the past, and present: the here and now, and the future. For our thoughts, ideas, opinions and views have a past, a foundation on which we build, or refuse to build on.

By learning the sociologies of other times, places and eras, including our own, the student gains some things of great value. The whole evolution, and at times revolution, process of human thinking against the backdrop of the times and places in which it occurred will inevitably change the student's own sociological cum philosophic and educational scene. The student's insight and horizon would broaden when s/he learns how others have viewed their lives; how they have attempted to solve their problems, how they have succeeded or failed. It is a different kind of experience. Through these 'journeys,' over the ages, the student finds that s/he starts to think sociologically, and philosophically, that is, to see the world and all its joys, problems and challenges in a different light. The physical conditions, the events encountered, the art, literature, technology, music, science, politics, ideology, economics, religion, the socio-culture, the education - in fact all the circumstances of one's existence - go to make up the sociological cum philosophical perspective. All these reflect back on the sociological foundations of education adopted.

We may start with a brief introduction to an era and sociology it deals with. The introductions will describe the circumstances and events that led up to, and were responsible for the representative thought of that age. There will follow a general survey of the chief exponents of that sociological thought, and of the major influences they have had on the education of their times and their regions. Then, only then do we examine the educational implications of sociological perspectives on educational and social issues, problems and challenges. I wish you luck, joy and tears as you embark on your sociological 'journeys,' and noble endeavours!

Tasks for reflection

In your own words, you may wish to explain the meaning of the term sociology.

It is also useful to analyze the essential qualities you would expect to find in an educated person.

The terms culture and society are among the most commonly used concepts in sociology. Culture refers to the ways of life of members of any given society, or of defined groups within society. It also refers to the learned, socially acquired traditions of thought and behaviour found in human societies. A society is viewed as a larger group of people with similar language, customs, values, social patterns and processes. So culture exists in society, and society live in culture. Though each human group has an overall culture, all societies contain smaller groups of people who have variations that are not shared by the rest of the society. So the variations in socio-cultural patterns and processes are referred to as subcultures. Examples of subcultures are groups based on class, religious or ethnic differences.

So, sociologists tend to use the term socio-culture, short for social and cultural patterns and processes, to indicate the complex system of interacting parts that link society and culture.

Types of Socio-Culture

There are common patterns and processes of a socio-culture that are universal. The cross-cultural recurrent aspects form a universal pattern. The universal pattern has three major divisions, namely structure, infrastructure, and superstructure.

Structure refers to the groups and organizations in society that allocate, regulate, and exchange goods, labour, data and information. These involve kinship and family relations; division of labour, socialization, age and gender roles, hierarchies, discipline, rewards and sanctions; political and economic organization for the whole society; provision and organization of religious rituals and educational activities; organization of reproduction and basic production, exchange, distribution and consumption within and outside society.

Infrastructure involves the technologies, productive and reproductive activities related to the provision of food, shelter, health; the satisfaction of sexual and procreative drives and needs; practices employed to maintain, expand or limit fertility, natality, mortality, nurturing and rearing of children. In other words, infrastructure involves all those processes and activities that affect us from the womb to the tomb. All these activities are viewed in the light of the opportunities and limitations placed on production and reproduction by the society's environment, ecosystems, and work patterns.

Superstructure consists of thought and behavioural processes that are related to symbols, meaning, art, music, dance, literature, beliefs, myths, religious rituals, games, hobbies, and values.

Another way of looking at socio-culture is the use of two broad categories, that is, material (physical) and metaphysical culture. Material socio-culture refers to all physical and material aspects of a people. It includes artifacts, architectural structures and patterns, goods, property, fauna and flora of value, minerals, land, water resources and so on. Scientific and technological discoveries and inventions form part of the material socio-culture. The same is true of writing, and studies like astronomy, science, mathematics, metallurgy and medicine.

Normally value, real and sentimental, is placed on the materials concerned. Rights, privileges, rituals and beliefs revolve around the material aspects so valued. This leads us to the second broad area, metaphysical socio-culture.

The term metaphysical is two words that have been coined. Meta means above, beyond, behind; and physical relates to matter, energy. So the word physical, concerns things that can be experienced through the five senses. Metaphysical socio-culture deals with ideas and issues that are beyond the physical, beyond the realm of the five senses. These are ideas and issues that are perceived through the mind or spirit.

Metaphysical socio-culture deals with the nature of existence, the nature of the person, and the nature of the world one lives in. It concerns itself with the person's origins, and where the person goes from here, the nature of the soul, the spirit and the mind. Religious beliefs, rituals, ceremonies, festivities, taboos, symbols and so on constitute metaphysical socio-culture.

Socio-Cultural Transmission, or Conveyance

Society and socio-culture form a complex system of interaction patterns and practices. As we have seen, the term society refers to an organized group of people who share a homeland, norms, values and necessities of life. Almost all societies, great and small, exhibit a socio-culture. In other words a socio-culture is universal. A fundamental sociological question is: How do societies develop and convey their respective socio-cultures? There are four possible ways of explaining and answering this question.

Enculturation is a process of passing socio-culture on from one generation to the next. So a socio-culture of a society tends to be the same from one generation to the next. Enculturation is consciously and unconsciously transmitted as older members of society invite, entice and even compel the young to adopt what they consider to be important socio-cultural patterns and practices. These form traditional ways of thinking and behaviour. However, enculturation fails to explain changes and shifts in socio-culture within the same society. Hence, societies have the generation gap problem. Margaret Mead (1970) touched the immortal problem of the generation gap thus

> *Today, nowhere in the world are there elders who know what the children know; no matter how remote and simple the societies are in which the children live. In the past there were always some elders who knew more than any children in terms of their experience of having grown up within a cultural system. Today there are none. It is not only that parents are no longer guides, but that there are no guides, whether one seeks them in one's own country or abroad. There are no elders who know what those who have been reared within the last twenty years know about the world into which they were born.*

Mead's concern is made more poignant with the explosion in knowledge and technology that is taking place in almost all societies. The world is fast shrinking in terms of technology and communication that it has become a global village. So ideas, inventions, ways of looking at things and issues get out of fashion very fast. So enculturation cannot explain all the variations in socio-cultural conveyance. So other explanations have to be found to account for the evolution, and revolution, of socio-culture.

Diffusion refers to the passing of socio-culture from a more influential society to another. It can be referred to as cross cultural hybridization, at times direct transplantation. Examples could be a conquering society, or a more influential society can affect the culture of another through its powerful appeal to the lesser society.

Osmosis is similar to diffusion but the process is from a less influential society to a more influential one. For example colonized people also influence the language, the habits, diets, and even thought processes of the colonizers. For example the Roman and Greek empires borrowed and adopted a lot of socio culture from the colonized peoples.

So most socio-cultural processes and patterns can be traced to another culture, another society. Diffusion and osmosis explain for socio-cultural differences and similarities. Most law, religion, governance systems, diets, language and habits have been borrowed from other socio-cultures. Judaeo-Christian religions have their origins in ancient Africa (Egypt and Nubia), then moved to the Middle East, then to Europe. Tea, now the centre of Western socio-culture had its origins in India. Legend has it that when tea was first brewed in England, the liquid part was thrown away and the leaves chewed instead. They ate tea rather than drank it. Tobacco came from the ancient Americas, and took the world by storm as a form of socio-cultural practice.

However, diffusion and osmosis fail to account why societies close to one another in space and environment retain different ways of life. Cosmopolitan societies in urban areas maintain their own socio-culture despite being close together. They continue to eat different foods, sport different clothes, practise different religions, speak different languages, in spite of their closeness. The African forest dwelling societies have lived for hundreds of years next to their agrarian neighbours. Nomadic groups have scurried around and about their more sedentary neighbours for centuries. Moreover, diffusion and osmosis cannot explain independent discoveries, inventions and practices by people in far distant places who have had no contacts with each other. So there must be some other way of explaining the socio-cultural phenomenon.

Sociologists have observed that there are socio-cultural patterns that are universal such as family, reproduction, raising children, organizing the exchange of goods and services, the use of signs and language. Simultaneous but independent discoveries and inventions have been made because the situation was ripe for them.

It may be prudent here to use a biological term to explain the socio-cultural phenomenon. Botanists have a relevant term called rhizome. Rhizome is the thick stem of certain plants that grows along or under the ground and has roots and shoots growing from it. A rhizome does not have to copy from another plant when to shoot, develop and grow. The environmental conditions have to be suitable for the growth processes to take place, regardless of differences in distance or space. So the same process takes place with human socio-culture producing varieties of universal patterns.

Rhizomery points to the fact that when the growing, interactive socio-cultural process reaches a certain point, an invention or discovery takes place. In other words when the cultural process has reached a critical point where an invention or discovery, or innovation becomes possible, that event becomes inevitable. Societies separate in space are likely to occupy similar environments, situations and challenges. Hence, the similarities between them may be caused by the effects of similar environmental conditions, and challenges. The world is so full of remarkable and striking instances in which societies, known never to have had any contact, invented similar tools, technologies, techniques as well as similar social practices.

It is useful to sum up this section by pointing out that socio cultural patterns, and processes are so complex that no single explanation suffices. The four explanatory principles help to explain ways in which socio culture is developed, conveyed within, across and outside societies. They complement each other in accounting for the variations and similarities of human life. It is true that cultures maintain continuity through the process of enculturation. Diffusion and osmosis come in handy to explain the process by which socio-culture is conveyed from one society to another. But the three cannot explain the similarities and differences with in, across and outside societies. Rhizomery is of great help in accounting for the simultaneity and multiplicity of socio-cultural occurrences. Some result from reactions to similar environmental conditions or situations and challenges.

Contexts of Socio-Culture

The universality and variations in socio-culture should make us appreciate the beauty, the richness and diversity of human life. This should lead us to a tolerance, and acceptance of socio-cultural differences and a willingness to learn more about them. This is important because there is need to avoid two negative phenomena called *ethnocentrism* and *xenocentrism*.

Ethnocentrism is the belief that one's own patterns of behaviour, way of life and culture are always natural, good, beautiful, superior and important. Strangers are regarded as having different, archaic, primitive, backward, disgusting, inhuman and irrational socio culture. This can lead to intolerance to socio cultural differences. This may lead to xenophobia, that is, a dislike or fear, and even hatred of foreigners. Hence many social strife, wars and clashes can be traced to intolerance and misunderstanding of socio cultures. A good example is that colonialism in Africa was justified on religious, legal, and humanitarian grounds. Humanitarian aid programmes today fund projects to improve the quality of life, providing health care, clean water, food, education, and other essential needs primarily in the developing world. They believe they share a vision of a better world. A lot of aid to developing countries is based on the need to develop a better life style, a better system and so on based on what the donor feels are basic socio cultural standards.

In recent times, calls for African ethnocentrism, a return to those core socio cultures of the African heritage, have become popular. These have sprung from the accession of the African countries to state sovereignty. Independence, freedom and liberation cut across political, ideological, economic, social and cultural divides. One over riding indispensable condition of independence has been the emergence of a country's socio culture on the local, regional and international scenes. This would be found in the flag, national anthem, national dress, national currency (no matter how worthless it is), traditional cuisine, national languages, literature, art, music and dance. The African personality is viewed as one that espouses the African heritage defined in historical, social and cultural terms. The African personality should shun neo colonialism with its foreign norms, values, languages, attire and social values. In other words, African socio culture should have a permanent place on the world plane as an equal among nations. Africa should remain itself, shaped and developed by its past and its people.

But there are those who fear that Africa might be helpless and left behind by the rest of the world. Africa should be able to live in the present and the future of the world. Africa has to participate in universal progress and integrate with modernization, and at the same time retain its own socio cultural heritage. It is a difficult balancing act to follow. So in the next paragraph we look at a different socio cultural point of view.

Xenocentrism is a term that comes from a Greek word xeno, which means foreign, from outside, not original. So xenocentrism is the belief that other people's patterns of behaviour, thought, language, material and metaphysical socio culture are better, more beautiful, more important, superior than one's own. This attitude is the opposite of ethnocentrism. Xenocentrism regards one's own socio culture as uncivilized, inhuman, disgusting, irrational, backward and unworthy of practice. This belief leads to a propensity for all things that are foreign at the expense of one's own socio culture. Good examples are colonized people who readily abandon their own socio culture and eagerly accept the colonizer's way of life: language, names, diet, ceremonies, festivals, dress, mannerisms, cosmetics, hair styles, religion, education, politics, laws, and creature comfort. All standards are measured and evaluated against the foreign socio culture. Because the person is not well versed in the foreign socio culture there is likely to be a mismatch resulting in exaggeration, misplaced emphasis and omissions that can become comical. Xenocentrism remains with a people long after the colonizers have left, leading to socio cultural neo -colonialism. Africa, in particular, is full of xenocentrism.

These socio cultural processes and practices are defended on the basis of modernity. One could not go to the past and live in the past. The world is now one, a global village. Africa benefits a lot from western technology, science, architecture, literature, communication systems, religion, art, music, attire and creature comfort.

As we have seen before, the universality and variations in socio-culture should make us appreciate the beauty, the richness and diversity of human life. This should lead us to a tolerance, and acceptance of socio cultural differences and a willingness to learn more about them. So sociologists, recognize the fallacy and negative implications of ethnocentrism and xenocentrism. The need to move towards tolerance of socio cultural differences, and a desire to learn more about the beauty and diversity of human life are at the very heart of sociological studies.

Socio Cultural Relativism

Sociologists place great emphasis on socio cultural relativism. Socio cultural relativism means that we should not pass judgement on the moral, legal and social worth of other people's socio cultures. No one has the monopoly, the absolute and the universal standards that can be used to rank socio cultural beliefs and practices as good, evil, acceptable or unacceptable. At most what could be done is to suspend any judgement about certain kinds of socio cultural beliefs and practices until thorough and convincing research evidence has been conducted.

Human experiences in different societies have a lot of lessons for us. Every society has common problems and challenges to overcome, for example, the problem of dependant members such as the very young and the very old. Solutions to such challenges are socio culturally determined so they vary from society to society.

Among western societies the very young, and the very old can be fostered through a net work of social institutions. Those too old to work are pensioned off and made to retire, and eventually die peacefully in geriatric homes. But amongst the Australian Natives, Eskimos, Caribou Indians and the San under harsh circumstances like famine, the killing of infants (infanticide?), and the killing of old people (geronticide?) were allowed to prevent the starvation of the whole community. First the active male adults would be fed because if they were too weak to hunt, everybody would starve. Next, their wives would be fed since they could bear more children. The very young, the very old and the infirm were expendable since they were a liability. At best they would be left behind to die. Some brave old people would commit suicide. It could also be argued that western societies also kill or allow people to die through modern practices such as vehicle accidents, plane crashes, factory mishaps, tobacco and alcohol abuse. All this could be interpreted as human sacrifice on the altar of development, progress, civilization, and ultimately the survival of the community. So the socio cultural differences are the same. The running theme seems to be survival of the community but it depends on which people.

Another interesting human experience is that surrounding sophistication. A San (Bushman) taken to the modern town for the first time would find it extremely difficult to find his or her way round the city with its mad metal lions, crazy riders, traffic jungle, weird flashing lights and confusing dripping pipes. Equally the town dweller taken to the Kalahari environment, would not know how to survive without water taps, without the doctor and chemist, without the supermarket, without the motorized transport. So in the different circumstances it is not possible to tell who is sophisticated. All this helps us to realize that human experience is relative.

Strongly related to socio cultural relativity is the relativity of science and truth. Here there are basically two opposing schools of thought. One endeavours to the search and discovery of universal truths emanating from the scientific enquiry. Through research and scientific investigation we reach the truth, be it physical or metaphysical. So whatever we study must subscribe to the rigors of the scientific method. Hence, scientific objectivity of phenomena should over ride personal feelings and nuances. The other school of thought says that objective facts and truths especially about human thought and action are unobtainable. Even those who use scientific methods could be biased by their own socio cultural background since they come from different localities, ethnic group, class, gender, nationality, even race.

Perhaps the most useful position to take is in the middle of the debate. Scientific objectivity means that we should endeavour to minimize the biases, the contaminating variables from influencing the results of the research study. Objective truth is temporary and provisional because more information is always surfacing where, and when we think we have arrived at the truth. After all, science involves a never ending, perpetual process of investigating, finding out phenomena about people and the world.

Socio Culture and Development

In today's technological world it is pertinent to highlight the role and place of socio culture in development. Before exploring in detail the implications of socio culture to development it is useful to revisit two inter connected definitions from Stoner et al (1995):

> *Socio culture is the complex mixture of assumptions, behaviours, values, norms, language, myths and other ideas that fit together to define what it means to be a member of a particular society; and on organizational socio culture the set of important understandings, such as norms, values, attitudes and beliefs shared by organizational members.*

In other words all of society has organizations, big and small. People live, work and recreate in groups that are, technically speaking, organizations. In this sense even a family unit can be an organization, just as a small or big company is. And these organizations can be corporations with strong socio cultures. Such socio cultures contribute either to the success or failure of enterprises. Organizations tend to develop innovative, at the same time, retain certain typical socio cultural characteristics. These tend to revolve around the three levels of socio culture, namely artifacts, espoused values and underlying assumptions.

Artifacts are things that come together to define a socio culture and reveal what it means to those who pay attention to them. Symbolism plays a very important part in artifacts and their place in society. Forms of dress such as uniforms, formal dress, suits, or jeans and the attitudes and behaviour towards them are part of artifacts. They extend to T shirts, logos, mottos, jargon, essential tools and equipment. All these can influence rapport, morale and productivity.

Espoused values are behind the reasons given by an organization for the way things are done. Organizations that are, or have been, under threat tend to develop a socio culture of safety, security, strictness and prudence. Those that have been around and have not experienced major disasters tended to develop a casual, relaxed, work and family socio culture.

Underlying assumptions are the beliefs that are taken for granted by members of an organization such as goals, technology, structure, perceptions, attitudes, feelings, values, formal and informal interactions. The major part of this level of socio culture is hidden or intangible. That is why it is called the iceberg of organizational socio culture. Or, to use an African expression, the ears of a hippo in water.

Hofstede (1984) and Ferreira (2000) provide useful analyses of different national cum organizational socio cultures. Socio cultural attitudes are related to nationality and the willingness to accept ideas. A full understanding of contemporary social life can be achieved by comparing and contrasting it with social life in other times and places. This is the comparative nature of sociology.

Socialization

A socio culture has two essential qualities: first it is learned, and second it is shared. Human beings rely for their survival on behavior patterns that are learned. The human infant is the most helpless at birth and cannot survive unaided. So, socialization is the process of making the infant become a self- aware, skilled and knowledgeable person in the socio cultural environment. Socialization is a life long process, but it is most profound in childhood. It would be interesting to see what would happen to an infant who remains unsocialized. There have been reported instances of unsocialized children.

It is reported (Haralambos and Holborn,1995) that Akbar, an Indian Emperor from 1542 to 1602 AD, ordered that a group of children be reared without any instruction in language, to test the belief that they would eventually speak Hebrew, the language of God. So the children were raised by deaf mutes. The children developed no spoken language and communicated solely by gestures.

There are also stories of children who were raised by wild animals. The most popular are those of the founders of Rome, Remus and Romulus who were suckled by a she wolf. There is also the story of the Wolf children of Midnapore. Two females, aged two and eight, were reportedly found in a wolf den in Bengal in 1920. They walked on all fours, preferred a diet of raw meat, they howled like wolves and lacked any form of speech. It is not clear whether these children had been raised by wolves or whether they had been abandoned and left to their own devices in the forest.

Shattuck, (1980) and Lane (1976) have a detailed report of the Wild Boy of Aveyron. It was on 9 January 1800 AD that a strange creature emerged from the woods near the village of Saint-Serin in the south of France. Though it walked erect, he looked more animal than human. He was soon identified as a boy of about eleven. He spoke only in shrill, strange sounding cries. He had no sense of personal hygiene and he relieved himself where and when he chose. The police took him to the local orphanage where he attempted to escape from. He refused to wear clothes. Doctors and specialists thoroughly examined him but no abnormalities were noted. A potato was held behind his head in front of a mirror and he tried to reach through the mirror to seize the potato he saw in it. A priest who observed the boy from day to day had this to say:

> *All these little details, and many others we could add, prove that this child is not without intelligence, reflection and reasoning power. However, we are obliged to say that, in every case not concerned with his natural needs or satisfying his appetite, one can perceive in him only animal behaviour. If he has sensations, they give birth to no idea. He cannot even compare them with one another. One would think that there is no connection between his soul or mind and his body...(Shattuck, 1980).*

The boy was later moved to Paris where there was not much success in making him more human. He accepted wearing clothes, he could use the toilet, but he was not interested in games. And more importantly he was never able to master more than a few words. Though there were no signs of mental retardation he seemed either unwilling or unable to master fully human speech. He died at the age of about forty in 1828.

It is difficult to make clear cut interpretations of this case since we do not have all the facts relating to the physiological and psychological conditions he was subjected to prior to his discovery. But past history and present events are full of reports of wild life rescuing humans in distress. The Biblical story of Jonah, having been thrown overboard by fellow humans ostensibly to drown, being rescued by a whale is well known. Stories of people shipwrecked being rescued from drowning and shark attacks by dolphins and whales are legendary. In 2004 a girl in Kenya was rescued by a set of lions from her human abductors. The lions only left her when game wardens appeared on the scene and took care of her. In 2008, a female dog was found nursing an abandoned human baby in the Natal sugar plantations. The dog would not leave the baby until it felt the baby was safe in hospital.

But one thing stands out clearly, from these accounts, that early socialization plays a pivotal role in developing human faculties as we know them. These reported cases indicate that prolonged and sustained socio cultural interaction with adults is necessary for proper human growth and development.

Religion and Socio Culture

Religion forms an integral part of society especially in Africa. Religious beliefs and practices form part of every day life. Mbiti (1987) asserts that those who pour libation to the gods, those who discuss their problems with their ancestors while walking, those who pray for success in the examination and those who carry a charmed bracelet ... all are carrying out religious practices. So too are those worshipers at Holy Communion, or those who face Mecca five times a day in prayer. A group thinks that they are descended from God, or gods, or a rock or tree. Some strongly believe they are descended from monkeys, cats, lions or zebras. Many people believe that their fate is not in their hands, but controlled by a supernatural power. These are all practices or acts of religion. Many authorities contend that no African is a true Christian or Moslem. They are eclectic in that they still believe in the influences of their socio culture. They have ancestral names, totems, praise names and beliefs in the powers of witchcraft.

The term religion comes from two Latin words: religio and religo. Religio means piety, sacredness, or fear of the supernatural. Religo means to bind or to fasten. From these two ideas, religion has come to embrace three aspects of social life. First, is the belief in supernatural powers, which are to be worshipped and obeyed. Second, is the social organization forms and practices which bind believers in a common sense of identity that originates in their acceptance as a group, of the correct way to think, feel and behave in religious matters. The third relates to attitudes and feelings of the believers (Bloom and Ottong, 1987). But religion does not have to involve beliefs in the supernatural per se'. Buddhism, for example, is concerned with meditation and reflection. To many sociologists, religion is regarded as one of the ways that people attempt to understand and cope with the ultimate problems of human existence. To many, religion gives them a philosophy of life, and a coherent view of how the social world moves. Marxists would regard religion as a form of escapism from the realities of life and human existence. It is the dream of the human mind. They would ask the question: Who created who? Is it God who created man, or man who created God?

Religion is a socio cultural system with its institutions and office bearers. It has a set of values, ideals and hopes that have meaning for the group. There is collective support and guidance for moral life. It is symbolic in that it offers solutions to hidden mysteries. The Holy Communion, or the Sacrificed Chicken, or Goat, stand for mystical relationships with God or Ancestors. Religions are also governed by emotions that Durkheim refers to as moods. The moods involve aspects of awe, reverence, truth about the world, and its future, and the Sect's triumph over others. The negative power of such moods is seen in religious wars, such as the Christian Crusades, Islamic Jihads, and sectarian violence.

Controversy in Religion

Besides having variations in religious types and forms, there is a lot of disagreements and controversy among religious groups. These differences range from dogma, doctrine, leadership, to processes and practices. Christianity has many sects though they all believe in Jesus Christ as the saviour. The Pope is revered by Roman Catholics but regarded with disdain by non Catholic Christians. The Christian Reformation was one of Christianity's biggest schisms that resulted in the fragmentation of the Christian church. Judaism has fundamentalists, the Pharisee, and the enlightened, the Saddusee who regard each other at variance to their religious laws, the sacred and the profane. Islam has its fundamentalists, the Shiite, and its enlightened group, the Sunnis.

With the exception of the Quakers, most religious organizations have clear divisions between the laity and the priesthood. The laity look to the priesthood to provide spiritual guidance, counseling, inspiration and the truth from the holy scriptures as interpreted by the priesthood. The priesthood leads in rites, ceremonies and festivals. The priesthood knows the religious secrets to put the worshippers into communion with God, or gods. In traditional African religion the priesthood revolves around the spirit- mediums and the chief. These tend to wield political, social and religious authority.

On the other hand it is pertinent to point out that more than half of the world's population does not believe in God, or supernatural power. Most of China, Japan and Asia do not believe in super natural powers as such. Many of them believe in the ideas of a personality such as Mao, Buddha, Confucius, and Zoroaster. This is clear evidence that people can live happily, and prosper, with no link to God, nor belief in super natural powers. They show more compassion and offer help to less fortunate people than their supernatural fearing counterparts. This is a major part of the paradox of religion and social life. Many social critics argue that religion is used as a social tool to dominate, hypnotize, indoctrinate and exploit the unsuspecting populace, especially the unsophisticated.

Religion and the Paradoxes of Power, and Entrepreneurship

Religious controversy, schism and change come mainly from the paradox of power, authority and influence. Weber's theory of power and authority comes handy here. The phenomenon of charisma resides in what Durkheim called the human fear of insecurity, unpredictable social world, which can be dangerous. Given such potential, and real unstable conditions people, like Freud's children, seek succour in a person of outstanding and extraordinary personal qualities. Charisma makes an individual, like Moses, Jesus, Mohammed, appear to be endowed with a supernatural, divine, personal magnetism. Weber noted three special social qualities of a charismatic leader. First, the quality is personal. It cannot be passed on to someone else. Second, charisma is a creative force. The person should move the followers to bring about far-reaching social changes in society. Third, charismatic leadership is spontaneous, and usually unpredictable. A charismatic leader appears when social stability has failed. The new leader is brave, visionary, and promises solutions to social and spiritual problems. The leader promises to lead the people out of danger, and into salvation. Should the leader fail there is always hope for yet another fresh saviour!

Because of the nature of social dynamics, charismatic leaders and their groups appear, and eventually disappear, especially in times of social, economic and political stress. Charismatic leaders are found all over the world. In Africa there are many straddling the social, religious, political and economic spheres. Trade union leaders have appeared in Southern Africa to hold political power and influence where nationalist movements have failed to deliver on socio economic promises. Together with the religious sects they pose a potential force for political and socio economic change.

Religious sects in particular experience fragmentation in Africa. As the leader fails to bring about the desired change or relief so will the authority and influence wane. The thousands of socio-religious prophets in Africa could be an indicator of Africa's crisis of governance and failure to deliver on desired expectations. It is also a sign of entrepreneurship on the part of the leaders of the emerging churches where the profit motive could be the driving force. Church members are made to give alms, gifts, property; to pay entry fees to healing and prophecy sessions. Members are also persuaded to buy books, CD's, DVD's, tapes, anointed apparel, raking in a fortune for the church, and its leadership.

The Rise of Millenarianism

Linked to the charismatic leadership style is the emergence of millenarianism. The term originally referred to sects that believed that Jesus Christ's rule of 1000 years was shortly to begin. So the Millenarian sects hold the view that a new social world is on the horizon, in which sinners will be punished, and believers will be triumphant. In this new world there will be no suffering, no injustice and no inequality. The world is divided into two: the believers who will be saved, and the non-believers who will be damned. These sects flourish in situations of social, economic and political stress. Hard pressed Africans turn to religion for solace. Their church membership in Africa is estimated at 30% of the population, and is rising. Christianity in Africa, mainly due to revival churches, is growing annually at the rate of 3.5% compared to 2.5% in Asia and Latin America and 1% in Europe and North America. Many of these sects, especially in Southern Africa, are beginning to focus on the growing awareness that their suffering does not emanate from above but from earthly based injustice, inequality and corruption. They are emerging as protest movements against new and indigenous socio-economic exploitation and political oppression. Post colonial regimes tend to be viewed as presiding over casino, and unpredictable, economies where winner takes it all.

The Fundamental Questions

For sociologists, the fundamental questions remain: How are influence, power and authority formed, retained and lost? How does leadership straddle the religious, social, political and economic divides? Weber's social organization theory tries to explain the social phenomena. True to form, religious organizations are partly concerned with fathoming the universe and their place in it. But they become also concerned with worldly social, economic and political issues and their place here on earth. Is it because man cannot live by bread alone?

Religious Metamorphosis

Humans are adaptable in many ways. Even religion has experienced metamorphosis. Change has come in many ways. Traditional religion in Africa has combined innovatively with Christianity. Christian churches, especially the Catholic Church, have blended traditional musical forms and instruments, local languages and ideas within Christian ritual and ceremony, into a new pattern. A Congolese Catholic mass, the *Missa Luba,* has a beautiful African and universal quality. In Latin America, Catholic saints have been integrated into local deities.

For sociologists the interest in religion centres on studying religion as one of the many social institutions found in society. Sociologists ask questions such as: How do people make sense of their social world? Why do groups invent supernatural powers to explain their world? Why do people have myths about the past to account for the present and to offer guidance for the future? Why are religious beliefs denied by many people, and a secular philosophy or ideology adopted in their place? Why are some people prepared to die or kill for their religious beliefs? How do people and groups change their religious beliefs? Examples are the Northern Ireland internecine between Catholics and Protestants, Islamic and Christian fights in Asia and North Africa, the Buddhist and secular repression in Nepal and China. Why are Traditional, Christian, Islamic and secular beliefs in competition especially in contemporary Africa? What are the effects of modern scientific and technological ideologies on social change? All these questions can form the basis of interesting studies on religion and socio culture. If you are looking for a research topic, the above questions could be very useful.

Chapter 3: Methods of Learning Sociology

Sociologists employ many kinds of methodology to learn about socio cultural patterns and processes. These include experiment, survey, observation, fieldwork, grounded theory, existing or past sources, censuses, interviews, questionnaires, life histories and genealogies.

Some of the questions sociologists ask in their research studies are largely factual and empirical. Comte and Durkheim believed that the scientific study of society should be confined to collecting information about social facts, that is, phenomena which can be objectively observed, interpreted, analyzed and classified. For example many social indices, sometimes called social facts, such as suicide, deaths, disease, divorce, marriage, literacy, crime rates need direct and systematic sociological investigation. A social index is an indication, preferably in statistical form, of the degree and incidence of a social event or occurrence. The sociologist could start by asking what forms of suicide are most common? Official statistics on suicide could be of help here. Interviews or questionnaires with appropriate authorities could shed some light.

Looking at the Social World in Different Ways

Social scientists try to make sense of social reality by looking at the social world in different ways. They may ask questions like: Why do people have different propositions about social reality? How do they view their social world? How can the truth they claim be discovered? In trying to find answers to these, and many more, questions sociologists take many stances, logics, models and techniques to study the social world. Ultimately these, and many, differences are based upon varied background assumptions (Hitchcock and Hughes, 1992). These assumptions are ontological, epistemological, methodological and technical.

Ontology refers to issues and ideas concerned with being. These concern issues surrounding the nature of humans, society and the social world. Epistemological assumptions refer to the questions of knowing and the nature of knowledge; the basis of knowledge, the form it takes, and the way it is transmitted. Methodology is concerned with the frames of reference, concepts, models, and ideas which shape the selection of a particular set of data gathering techniques. It is at this stage that decisions are made on whether to collect quantitative or qualitative data. Technical issues relate to equipment, tools and techniques through which the researcher carries out the study. The researcher makes technical assumptions about the practicality and appropriateness of certain techniques and instruments for the study. The basic ontological and epistemological assumptions held by a researcher would determine the methodology adopted.

Hitchcock and Hughes (1992) sum up the relationship between the set of assumptions diagrammatically thus:

Ontological Assumptions will give rise to
   \
    Epistemological Assumptions which have
       \
        Methodological Implications for the choice of particular
          \
           Techniques of Data Collection

Quantitative and Qualitative Data

The scientific method presupposes empirical evidence. Empirical evidence is easy to come by when dealing with things, matter, fauna and flora. One could choose the objects of experimentation, capture the objects, control the variables, and experiment with little concern for ethical considerations. Resultant evidence could be quantified in form of mathematical and statistical data. But with humans it is difficult to deal with them the scientific model. Attempts to manipulate them would almost result in the subjects counter manipulating the researcher resulting in contaminated evidence. Good examples come from the psychology of testimony area. People would swear under oath to tell the truth but proceed to make omissions and commissions of perjury. Opinion polls and economic forecasts miss their targets. In everyday life people tell others what they think the people want to hear.

Because of these, and other, reasons there have been fierce differences between those who favour the scientific model, with its quantitative data, and those who support the interpretive method that advocates qualitative data. You have to make up your mind on which type of data you are comfortable with. The emphasis here is on verifiable, accurate, reliable and valid evidence.

Empirical and factual data do not tell the sociologist all about a social phenomenon in society. So the sociologist may ask comparative questions relating to one social situation to another or contrasting examples from different social groups. Sociologists may want to understand the nature of societies, past, present and future. Or the sociologist may decide to observe the social situation or event by either passively or actively being involved. Sociologists use the term passive observation and participant (active) observation respectively.

How well these theories are explained, the subtlety of the arguments and the quality of the evidence, will vary by author or researcher. It is also dependent on the conviction and arguments of the source which is more often grounded in what is considered reason and fact. In distilled form, though, the explanations of different views become mirror images of each other. However, like all good theories they contain enough truth to, at least, satisfy those predisposed to believe in them, without admitting any contradictions that may shake up those assumptions. Their purpose may not necessarily be to persuade the other side but to keep their bases assured of the rightness of their respective positions. All this may be disconcerting to the student of social sciences.

But of course, there is social reality revealed in the millions of people who go about their business everyday. They are on the job, or looking for work, starting businesses, having visions of fair wages and benefits. They may be looking for school places for their children, or involved in patronage or punishment. Some prefer tradition, norms, value or social experimentation. Life is about the knowledge, values, attitudes, and traditions that guide behaviour, and actions, of a group of people. These allow them to solve problems of living in their environment. They may be struggling with energy and water provision, insufficient health cover, and a pension that cannot meet the basic necessities. So they are by turns hopeful and frightened about the future. Instead they turn to skepticism, agnosticism, politics, or religion and other ideologies. In other words, their lives are full of contradictions and ambiguities. That is life as experienced by people.

Out of all this there is need to understand themselves as humans, their place on earth and the universe; the land of warring factions and ethnic hatreds. Out of it, despite all these differences, comes the imperative to examine and understand just how much they share common hopes, dreams, problems, and form a bond that will not break. That is the task, the aim and objective of a student of social science.

The Concept Research

Sociologists also use the term research to describe a systematic inquiry into a social problematic situation. Research normally has a prefix to it, for example, basic research, pure research, applied research. Basic research deals with mundane and fundamental principles of investigation, usually for beginners. Pure research is concerned with advancing knowledge within a particular discipline. Applied research is concerned with developing understanding of practical problems in specific situations. It may take an inter-disciplinary format.

It is pertinent to point out that whatever methodology a sociologist uses it must be credible, verifiable, valid and reliable. Reliability is the degree to which a test produces consistent results over several administrations. Validity is the degree to which a test measures what it claims to measure. Good sociological work avoids generalizations, commonsense speculation, jumping to conclusions and using sweeping statements. The sociologist tries to make questions as precise as possible and seeks to gather as much accurate evidence as s/he can, interpret and analyze it before coming to conclusions.

Research Procedure

When carrying out a sociological study there are variations but the following is the usual procedure:
- Define the Problem, that is, ask the question, then select a topic for research
- Review related literature, familiarize yourself with existing studies on topic
- Formulate statement, that is, what do you intend to find out, any variables
- Select a method, e.g. survey, observation, existing sources
- Select instrument, e.g. questionnaire, test, interview;
- Indicate and justify population, sample, and sampling procedure;
- Carry out the study, i.e. collect data, record information, cross check them;
- Interpret and analyze your results or findings, work out implications of data
- Report the study findings, their significance, relations to other findings
- Register your findings, at workshops, conferences, seminars, in journals

Selecting Research Methodology

In selecting method of study one has to bear in mind its strengths and limitations. A summary of some of the main methods used in sociological study would be of help here.

Method	Details
Experiment	
	Strengths • Influence of specific variables can be controlled by investigator; • Easier for subsequent researchers to repeat or replicate *Limitations* • Many aspects of social life cannot be studied under laboratory conditions. The responses of subjects under study may be affected by the experimental situation, which could be artificial
Correlation	
	Strengths • Researcher explores the relationships between two or more variables that exist naturally and tries to sort out what goes with what. Examples are smoking and disease, intelligence and creativity, socio economic status and achievement. Many studies that show strong relationships between certain features of classroom, and school management and learning are nearly all correlational. *Limitations* • Correlational research does not establish cause and effect among variables, only relationships. The research method lacks the exactness and veracity of the experiment.
Causal-Comparative	
	Strengths • It is used to explore causal relationships, with the independent variable not manipulated. Data are used from already defined groups. Researcher compares two groups for whom a particular trait or pattern exists, and for whom it is absent. Differences between means and effects are compared. The statistical tests are similar to those used in experimental research. This differs from correlational studies, in which the correlation coefficient is observed. *Limitations* • Like the correlational research, causal-comparative studies are limited, and must be interpreted with care because it is not clear whether the variables are a cause, effect, or a result of other factors.
Observation	
	Strengths • Can generate richer and deeper information than other methods • Provides flexibility for the researcher to change and follow new leads *Limitations* • Can only be used to study relatively small groups or communities • Findings might only apply to the groups or communities studied
Survey	
	Strengths • Efficient collection of data on large numbers of individuals possible • Precise comparisons can be made between the answers of respondents *Limitations* • Material gathered may be superficial; important differences between

Method	Details
	• Respondents' responses may be glossed over; difficult to determine the veracity of the responses
Documentary	
	Strengths • Provides authentic sources of data on large numbers or population • Ideal for studies that are historical in nature *Limitations* • Researcher depends on the existing sources, which could be partial, audited and secondary sources, e.g. statistics, could be difficult to interpret in relation to real tendencies or happenings
Ex Post Facto	Sometimes referred to as causal-comparative research
	Strengths • Aims to describe conditions which already exist e.g. major causes of cancer – smoking link; development of bottle fed and breast fed babies; • Attempts to explain the reasons or causes for the phenomenon under study; inferences about the relationships among variables are made without direct intervention • Systematic and empirical inquiry in which independent variables have already occurred *Limitations* • Variables impossible or unethical to manipulate • Researcher deals with the social facts determined already
Action Research	Is an inquiry conducted into a particular issue of current concern, Usually undertaken by those directly involved e.g teachers
	Strengths • Aims at using results/ findings to implement change in a specific situation. It is favoured by Care Givers, project developers • Focuses on a specific problem, in a specific setting. It is action oriented targeting specific objectives. *Limitations* • Those directly involved in a situation may lack insights into the real causes of the problems; they may lack the outsider perspective. There can be the tendency to confirm what one wants to find out.
Grounded Theory	Is a research method that is developed as the researcher conducts the study in the field. Questions, instruments, variables and samples come out as a result of what transpires in the field of investigation. The basis for grounded theory is that truth only reveals itself when one gives up all preconceived ideas before embarking on the research.
	Strengths • It allows for flexible, accurate and reliable development of instruments depending on reality on the ground. It avoids preconceived assumptions, bias and wrong views before hand *Limitations* • It can be cumbersome in that one has to move in and out of the field to consult experts and advisers, breaking the continuity and flow of gathering data. There are dangers of going native, that is, data could be contaminated by taking sides and having sympathies with the researched.
Case Studies	A case study involves a detailed study of a single institution, social group, an individual person, a single social action, or a particular socio historical event. Life histories are a particular type of case study concerning an individual's life. It utilizes interviews, observations, biographies, personal or individual life situations.

Method	Details
	Strengths
	• Case studies can be used to arrive at comprehensive understanding of the subject under study. They can also be used to develop more general theoretical frameworks in social structure and processes; or to generate new hypotheses which can then be tested against data, or later studies. It is also flexible in the use of methods. They can also be used to confirm, or falsify a general theory about life. Case studies are also useful to produce a typology, i.e. a set of categories defining types of a social phenomenon.
	Limitations
	• Major draw backs of case studies are that it is difficult to generalize on the basis of findings. The data are particular study fixed and oriented.
	• It is very difficult to relate, or apply, a social phenomenon to later, or earlier studies. The study cannot be repeated with similar subjects otherwise the research ceases to be a case study

So, each of the various methods of study has its strengths and limitations. For this reason it is prudent to combine two or more methods, each being used to supplement or check the data obtained from the other. All the same a researcher has to find own comfort zone regarding theory, method and instruments. The most common forms of research instruments centre on opinionnaires (opinion polls, questionnaires, interview schedules). These are information sheets or forms that attempt to measure the attitudes, beliefs, and views of individuals so that a sample of their opinions is obtained.

Ethical Considerations

A word of warning is needed here. Social science study often presents the researcher with ethical dilemmas. These could arise from the publication of findings that might adversely affect the person, the lives, or feelings of those studied. So all researchers have to be extra sensitive to the ethical dilemmas they could pose or cause.

Hence, there should be informed consent by the respondents, preferably in writing. Gray (2004) says the following are critical ethical concerns for the researcher. The researcher should explain the purpose of the enquiry to the researched. There should be clear promise and reciprocity as to the benefits and social rewards accruing from the study. Data access and ownership should be clarified as to who has the right to access data and for what purpose. There should be risk assessment regarding possibilities of danger to the respondents, for example, political repercussions, legal liabilities, social ostracism, health implications. Hence confidentiality of data is critical. The researcher will know but will not divulge under any pressure or circumstances. It is the same confidentiality that exists between a priest and confessing person, or doctor and patient.

Descriptive Statistics and Research

A chapter on research methods should have a section on descriptive statistics. Descriptive statistics complement descriptive research. Descriptive statistics attempt to gather detailed information about some phenomenon and sum it up in a short version, statistically. Research findings should be statistically significant and not a chance occurrence. Descriptive statistics belong to measurement and evaluation. It is evaluation expressed in quantitative, numerical, terms. There are a number of measurement instruments. These range from norm referenced tests, to criterion referenced tests. Norm referenced testing is where scores are compared with the average performance of others. There are at least three forms of comparison groups referred to as norm groups. A class or school can be used as a norm group. A district or cluster of schools is another form of comparison group. The nation can be used as a norm group. Organizations like UNESCO can use groups of countries as a comparison group. Norm referenced tests work best when measuring general ability in certain areas like history, languages and general knowledge. They are also useful when assessing the range of ability of large groups, in an effort to select top candidates, when only a few openings are available.

Criterion referenced testing is when scores are compared to a set performance standard. Criterion referenced tests measure the mastery of specific tasks and objectives. The results of the test should tell the researcher exactly what an individual can do, or cannot do, under certain specified conditions. Examples are driving licence examinations, operations of specialized equipment and aircraft flight tests. So criterion referenced measuring instruments work best when measuring mastery of specific skills. They can also be used to determine if learners have prerequisites to start on new work; or to group individuals for instruction. They are essential for assessing affective and psychomotor outcomes.

Standardized tests are a result of tests given nationwide under uniform conditions, and scored according to uniform procedures. They are based on a large sample, called a norming sample, of people serving as a comparison group for scoring standardized tests.   There are a number of measurements on which comparisons, and interpretations are made.

Frequency distribution is simply a listing of the number of people who obtain each score, or fall into each range of scores on a test, or other measuring device. It is a record showing how many scores fall into set groups. A graph, bar graph, or histogram is used to express the results. Usually a simple line graph is used where one axis, the x or horizontal axis, indicates the possible scores, and the other axis, the y or vertical axis, indicates the number of people who attained each score.

Standardized tests also involve measurements of central tendency and standard deviation. Central tendency is a typical score for a group of scores. Standard deviation is a measure of how widely scores vary from the mean. Measures of central tendency are the mean, median and mode. A mean is an arithmetic average of a group of scores. To calculate the mean one adds the scores and divide the total by the number of scores in the distribution.

The median is the middle score in a group of scores, or in the distribution. This is at the point at which half the scores are larger, and half are smaller. The mode is the most frequently occurring score. It is the score that occurs most often. If the frequency distribution has two modes it is called a bimodal distribution.

Measures of central tendency give a score that is representative of the group of scores but they do not tell anything about how the scores are distributed. So the standard deviation comes in handy. It is a measure of how widely the scores vary from the mean. The larger the standard deviation, the more spread out the scores in the distribution. On the other hand, the smaller the standard deviation, the more the scores are clustered around the mean. Standard deviation needs some algebraic calculations using square roots to find the average. First, the mean of the scores is calculated, written as μ. The mean is subtracted from each of the scores, written as $(X-\mu)$. Each difference is squared by multiplying each difference by itself. This is written as $(X-\mu)^2$ All the squared differences are added, written as $\sum(X-\mu)^2$. This total is divided by the number of scores, written as

$$\frac{\sum(X-\mu)^2}{N}$$

Then the square root is found using the standard deviation formula for calculating.

Standard deviations are very useful in understanding results, especially if the results are plotted on a normal distribution curve. Normal distribution is the most commonly occurring distribution, in which scores are distributed evenly around the mean. The normal distribution is a bell shaped curve, sometimes referred to as Napoleon's hat. It has certain predictable characteristics. Usually 68% of the scores are clustered within 1 standard deviation below, to 1 standard deviation above, the mean.

The normal distribution curve can be used to translate one type of standard score into another. Standard scores are based on the standard deviation. A common standard score is the Z score. It indicates the number of standard deviations above, or below, a mean. To calculate the Z score of a given raw score, the mean is subtracted from the raw score, and the difference is divided by the standard deviation. The formula is

$$Z=\frac{X-\mu}{SD}$$

Some people find it cumbersome to use the Z score formula especially the negative numbers, so the T score is used. A T score is a standard score with a mean of 50, and a standard deviation of 10. To eliminate the decimal, the Z score is multiplied by 10. To get rid of the negative number 50 is added. The answer is the equivalent T score. A Z score of -1.3 would translate to 37.

As -1.3 x 10= -13

Therefore -13 + 50= 37

Another widely used standard score is the stanine score. Stanine stands for standard nine. There are only nine possible scores on the stanine scale. They are whole number scores from 1 to 9, each representing a wide range of raw scores. The mean is 5, and the standard deviation is 2. Each stanine score represents a wide range of raw scores. This encourages stake holders to view individual scores in more general terms.

Yet another standard measure is correlation, which deals with how two or more variables are related. A variable is a characteristic of a physical or social situation that can change, or vary from one instance to the other. In other words, correlation is a statistical description of how closely two variables are related. There is the independent variable and the dependent variable. The independent variable is treated, and presumed, to cause some change in the dependent variable. On the other hand, the dependent variable may change as a result of the independent variable, that is, the consequences of the independent variable on the dependent variable. The dependent variable depends on the independent variable.

In correlation research the correlation coefficient are numbers ranging from +1.00 to -1.00 that describe the numerical relationship between variables. In an animal, for example, the place where there are horns, one finds, in another animal, horns of the same shape and size, the correlation coefficient is +1.00, positive correlation. But if one finds in the same place a set of ears the correlation coefficient is -1,00, negative correlation. If, on the other hand, one finds nothing in the same place, then there is 0, that is, no correlation.

More information on measurement, evaluation and assessment can be found in Woolfolk(2001), and Arends (1994).

A student of social science should endeavour to use measures and tests with caution. They do not necessarily tell the whole story about people and situations. The aim is to use measures to try to unravel social behaviour, action and processes as accurately as humanly possible. Research is about finding more knowledge surrounding social, economic, natural and environmental phenomena. A good research, like a good experiment, raises more questions than it answers. A good research should try to find solutions to real life problems.

Information Technology and Communication for Social Science Study

Students of social science should not only keep abreast of technological developments, but be ahead, beyond the horizon as it were. It is pertinent to note that information technology and communication has its origins in space travel, military expeditions, espionage techniques and geopolitical interests. It has recently found applications in sciences, commerce, industry and education. Because of it, the world is now connected with the global networks turned into multi million money enterprises. The digital super highway spans the world at lightning speed. When one looks at the digital world map mounted on a screen at Google, one is struck by the light generated by internet searches coming from every corner of the world. World broadband deployment and high speed internet dominate Japan, Europe, America, and some Asian countries. Huge parts of Africa are dark, with strands of internet light shining here and there. This tells a story of poverty and absence of internet connectivity and activity. Wireless spectrum and speed broadband access should connect schools, libraries, homes, hospitals and other social facilities if Africa is to develop. Students of social sciences should take the lead in this academic endeavor. So a basic understanding of information technology and communication is essential.

Internet Source

Internet sources come in two forms, general search engines and meta search engines. General search engines are Ask, Bing, Google, Google Scholar, MSN, Yahoo. Meta search engines are Ithaki, Lxquick, Surfwax, Vivismo, Webcrawler. All these sources offer academic, research, social and knowledge services

Internet Services

Internet services cover a wide area of operations. E-mail is for general communication purposes such as writing and posting letters, document delivery. Staff and student portals are for conferencing, tutoring and sharing knowledge bases. News groups share news, experiences and information.

E-Resources

These are concerned with electronic teaching, learning, publishing and exchange of academic work. There are e-journals, e-books, e-encyclopaedia, e-dictionaries. These resources are invaluable as desk top, home, library, at a flick of a button or mouse.

Course Management Systems

These are blog, or chat online management systems for designing course outlines, content, tutoring, marking and feedback. They can be used for applying online resources such as uploading and downloading files. They can be used for virtual class applications by integrating audio and video conferencing, and updating teaching/learning materials. They can be used for understanding new techniques such as computer language e.g HTML. They can also be used for data base applications such as data input, sorting records, Microsoft access.

Internet Tools

These are used for presentations, lecture delivery such as Power Point, content specific such as Wiki Space, Moodle; for communicating such as audio/video conferencing, student portals for designing courses, giving work, tests, marking and assessing. These tools can be used for accessing educational, teaching and learning materials. Web tools are useful for sharing knowledge, ideas and skills. The tools are also used for publishing e-journal articles, e-books and so on.

Internet for Social Networking

These social chat circles, or rooms, are used for social purposes, video conferences to share current news, events, pictures and contemporary issues. Examples of these social networks are Bing, Facebook, Skype, Twitter, WhatsApp.

With this world of information technology, coupled with cellular mobile phones and digital satellite, the global village is accessed almost immediately. The frontiers of communication, knowledge, ideas and skills are within reach of the social science student, in particular, and people in general.

Referencing Conventions and Techniques

A chapter on methods of studying sociology should end with a section on referencing conventions and techniques. A student of sociology is expected to make the correct, and consistent, citation of sources in formal academic writing. The citing of references is an important part of social research. It is a good indication of the researcher's ability to locate suitable, and relevant, sources, and to use the ideas to support own views and conclusions. The correct, and consistent, bibliographic details should be given in such a way as to make the sources easily traceable and identifiable. There are many conventions but the rules of thumb are to use one that is wanted by your institution, and to use it consistently. Stringer (1984) insists that the lay out and the content of bibliographic information should be given correctly. He believes that the correct format would not only help the student to write references correctly but enable the student to provide the correct information when asking for resource materials from a library or ordering publications for purchase.

The student needs to be aware of the differences in format, arrangement and intent of publications such as encyclopedias, dictionaries, institutional reports, journals, monographs, newspapers, yearbooks. The student should also know how different types of publications come into print. The process involves authorship (individual, joint, corporate), function of editors, compilers, works written as part of a series, the role of the publisher (and a second publisher), the role of the printer, reasons for copyright, reprints, new editions, impressions. (Stringer, 1984).

Agreed General Guidelines on Referencing

As indicated above, there are many referencing conventions. But what is important is to be consistent. But there are agreed general guidelines. The term bibliography is used as the heading for a list of sources appearing at the end of the work, but not referred to in the text. Many authorities do not like this as there is no evidence to show that the sources have actually been used. The term, references is used as the heading for a list of sources appearing at the end of the work, to which reference has been made in the text. Footnotes can be used for explanatory or elaboratory notes which are not desired as part of the text.

Footnotes can also be used as brief references to sources used, the full details of which will appear in a list of references. Footnotes can also be used as complete references to sources used, where no list of references appears at the end of the work. When using footnotes there are common abbreviations used. Examples are ibid which is short for ib-idem, a Latin adverb, meaning in the same book, article, passage; op cit, Latin opere citato, meaning in the work already quoted or cited; loc cit, Latin locere citato, meaning in the work already located, or as indicated. So the word citation comes from Latin, the language of the Roman Empire. Because of its brevity and conciseness Latin is used in academic and professional studies such as sciences, medicine and law.

Citation in the text is the way in which sources are referred to in the body of the text depending on convention used. The student should find out from the authorities in the institution on what to use. What is important is that the student does not mix ways of citing sources.

A Guide to Bibliographic Description of Sources
A useful guide to the bibliographic description of sources is given by Gates (2001).

One author
Bieler, Ludwig, Ireland. *Harbinger of the Middle Ages.* New York: University Press, 1963.

Two authors
Brown, James, W. , and Norberg, Keneth, D. *Administering Educational Media.* New York: McGraw-Hill Book Company, 1975.

Several authors
Davis, Cullom, et alia (and others). *Oral History: From Tape to Type. Chicago*: American Library Association, 1977.

Organization or institute as author
American Institute of History and Art. *Hudson Valley Painting, 1700-1750.* Albany, N.Y.: Albany Institute of History and Art, 1969.

Edition of an author's work
Deutsch, Babette. *Poetry Handbook: A Dictionary of Terms. 4th ed.* New York: Funk & Wagnalls Company, 1974.

Author's work edited by another person
Cary, Joyce. *Selected Essays.* Edited by A.G. Bishop. New York: St. Martin's Press, 1976.

Translation
Chastel, Andre. *The Age of Humanism: Europe, 1480-1530.* Translated by Katherine, M. Delavenay and E.M. Gwyer. New York: McGraw-Hill Book Company, 1963.

Edited work
Smythe, Mabel M. (ed.). *The Black American Reference Book.* Englewood Cliffs, N.J.: Prentice-Hall, Inco. ,1976.

Volume in a series
Lunt, William Edward. *History of England.* 4th ed. (Harper's Historical Series). New York: Harper & Brothers, 1957.

Encyclopaedia signed and unsigned
Seligman, Edwin R.A. "what are the Social Sciences?" Encyclopaedia of the Social Sciences, I, 3-7. "Phoenicia." *The Encyclopaedia Americana* XXI (1958), 786-788.

Periodical article
Trippett, Frank. "The Weather: Everyone's Favorite Topic." *Time*, CXI (February 6, 1978), 76-77.

Essay, Article, or Chapter in a collected work
Morgan, E. "Women and the Future." *In Images of the Future: The Twenty-first Century and Beyond*, pp. 143-151. Edited by R.F.Bundy. Buffalo, N.Y.: Prometheus Books, 1976.

Newspaper
Jonas, Jack. "A visit to a land of many facets," *The Sunday Star* (Washington, D.C.), March 5, 1961, sec. F, p.1.

Internet
http://www.wikiLeaks.org/wiki/main-page

Theories of Society

The previous sections introduced us to some of the basic concepts used by many sociologists. We have been presented with what appears to be a one-sided view of human society and behaviour. The impression given was that all people are commonly socialized, share a common agreed socio culture, share a common set of values, norms, statuses as they play and perform their roles. The impression given was that there is conformity to a common culture.

This appears to be so because most of these sociological terms derive from one dominant perspective, that is, functionalist theory of society. The other reason for this fallacy is that the first sociologists like Comte, and Durkheim were basically functionalist in orientation. Even those who belong to the conflict perspective like Karl Marx and Max Weber also used similar terms.

So it is important to point out that there are many sociological perspectives, each leading to different pictures and portraits of the social world. We should look at each theory to identify the relevance and usefulness in describing and explaining social behaviour. We should appreciate how different perspectives could be complementary as well as contradictory. Complementariness and contradiction are the essence of life that brings out the dialectical nature of society. Dialectics can be found in biology as female and male, in physics positive and negative, in mathematics plus and minus, in religion believer and pagan, in social sciences hero and villain. So the laws of dialectics make life and social dynamics so exciting and painful. We should use these different theories as tools to study, describe, interpret, explain and analyze the social world, no matter their differences.

The kinds of study that sociologists carry out and the kinds of conclusions they stress are greatly influenced by the basic assumptions they make about human life, and society. Basic assumptions and beliefs made by sociologists of different theoretical persuasions are called sociological paradigms, or theories. Sociology can be viewed as a way of thinking about the social world rather than an endeavour to find the truth or the one correct explanation. There are many different ways of studying, looking at, interpreting, analyzing and explaining systems we see, the actions of others, and the social world. Each view- point, or perspective, or orientation is based on different starting assumptions about how the social nature of the world is established, maintained, and how individuals and groups operate within that particular world.

Sociological perspectives are theories of society. A theory is a set of ideas that endeavours to explain how and why something works. Hence, a sociological theory is a set of ideas that claims to give an explanation of why, and how society, or aspects of society, work.

Sociological theories can be classified into two broad categories called macro and micro theories. In our experience of life we inhabit, simultaneously, different worlds. We inhabit the micro (small) world of our immediate experience with others as we interact with them. At the same time we inhabit a macro (big) world with much larger structures and institutions involving us with others removed from us by size and distance. So the microscopic and the macroscopic views of life, groups and society present to the sociologist a full picture of social life. That is why sociologists also talk of microsociology, that concentrates on small groups, face to face interpersonal relations and individual interactions. Macrosociology deals with the study of large scale social structures, major institutions and their interrelations within whole societies.

The macro social world refers to the large institutions which constitute society such as education, political, economic, and legal systems. Thus macro sociology concerns itself with the study and analysis of large scale social systems and how they are interrelated. From these macro theories individuals and groups are seen as fitting into society as it exists. So, people are viewed as external to their day to day activities. The ways in which people live their every day lives are to a large extent affected by institutional framework.

The micro social world looks distinct from the macro world but in reality the two are closely connected as we shall see later. The micro social world refers to the immediate world of our interpersonal relations and interactions with others. So micro-sociology studies face-to-face interaction of all forms of social organization, big and small. Here the analysis is interested in analyzing how the interactions of active and passive members shape and reform the nature of the social worlds which they inhabit. Micro analysis is concerned with people's interpretation of their social world, that is, how they give meaning to their social world. In other words society is seen as the construction of the collective actions of the people who constitute it.

We look at *Functionalist, conflict cum Marxian*, theories. These theories are sometimes referred to as the systems perspective because they look at societal systems as a whole.

Functionalism

Functionalism is an all encompassing theory of society that covers a wide area called the *consensus* perspective. Emile Durkheim was the most influential of the early functionalists. He is the guru of this perspective. He believed that, just as biologists would look at the living organism's parts and how they relate and function, the various parts of society were interrelated and should be taken together as a complex complete system. So to understand any part of society, for example, the family or religion, that part should be seen in relation to society as a whole (organic order). Just as the biologist would examine a part of the body in terms of its contribution to the maintenance of the human organism, the functionalist examine a part of society, or an aspect of it, in terms of its contribution to the maintenance of the social system. So all the organs of society, or aspects of it, must be methodically and thoroughly examined.

Structure

Functionalists (Durkheim, Parsons etc) start with the observation that behaviour in society is structured. Social relationships are organized, patterned and recurrent. Values provide general guidelines for behaviour with norms and roles directing specific actions. Institutions such as the family, educational systems, economic and political systems are major elements of social structure. Social relationships within the institutions are structured in terms of a set of related functions, norms, roles and values. A branch of functionalism called *structural functionalism* concentrates on studying society through its structures. Functions, roles, norms, values etc are examined and studied through the institutional structure.

Function

Functionalists, after establishing the institutional social structure, proceed to study the purposes and functions of the identified structures. The relationship between the different parts of the structure, their link and relationship to society are then examined. The contribution an institution makes to the survival and maintenance of the social system is an integral part of functionalist analysis (Cosin, 1972).

Functionalism is guided by establishing basic requirements or needs to be met for a social group to survive. These they call functionalist pre-requisites. Examples are: food, shelter, clothing, transportation and communication. Thus a major function of the economic system is the production and maintenance of the prerequisites. Hence, schools, teachers (education system) are viewed as performing the socializing function of members of the social group into the socio-economic system. Parsons identified *four prerequisites*: adaptation, goal attainment, integration, latency. Latency or pattern maintenance, is concerned with tension and stress management. Functionalists also talk of functional imperatives. These are the basic problems with which all social systems should cope with if the system is to be maintained. The four basic problems of a social system are: adaptation to other systems and the physical environment; attainment of system goals and mission statements; integration of the parts of the social system; and the maintenance of stability and management of internal tensions.

Merton further expands on functions by bringing in the concepts of manifest and latent functions. Manifest functions are those consequences of social behaviour that are both intended and recognized by participants in the social system. For example, streaming in a school as a policy is intended to make learners learn according to their levels of ability. Latent functions are not intended nor recognized consequences of social behaviour. The example given above of streaming could have the unintended consequences of anti school attitudes and behaviour. As latent functions become apparent institutions within society make adjustments to accommodate or counter the consequences of particular societal arrangements. So, social change could be explained through the concepts of manifest and latent functions of societal practices.

Functionalists brought in the notion of dysfunction also as a way of explaining change. Dysfunction refers to the consequences of any actions that disrupt, limit, or lessen stability and cohesion of the particular society. These are actions that upset the equilibrium of a supposedly smooth functioning society.

Consensus

From a functionalist perspective, consensus is a general agreement about functions, norms, values and roles by members of a society or social group. So consensus is a major tool for resolving conflicts and contradictions. Incidents of conflict only surface to be resolved through agreement on those aspects that are compatible and can be integrated. So the educational process endeavours to socialize members of society into harmonious relationships and conformity to norms, values and roles. Conflict is seen as a result of temporary turbulence in the social system that are normally resolved through negotiation and finding common areas of agreement, in other words, consensus. Though social groups can have differences of interests these are minor compared to the interests that all social groups share and cherish. Society as a whole benefits from a well structured, organized and peaceful system with agreed and shared values, norms, roles, needs and interests. That is why this theory is sometimes referred to as the normative perspective.

Social Order

Functionalists assume that order, harmony and stability are essential for the survival of social groups or systems. Again, consensus (agreement) on common culture forms the basis of social unity (*social solidarity*) as people share the same values. So *value consensus* provides the basis for cooperation since a common shared culture produces common goals. So consensus vis-à-vis social order is maintained through the institutionalization of a common culture with its attendant requisites: harmony, order and stability. The family, and later the school, are seen as vital parts of the social structure that help to socialize, inculcate and maintain social control and social order (Parsons, 1937).

Criticisms of the Functionalist Perspective

Being the first and oldest theory of society, this perspective has had a lot of criticism, especially when applied to education. We summarize here some of the criticisms that have been made. First, a look at society would suggest that conflict is present as often as consensus. Conflict is more characteristic of present day world than are consensus, cohesion and integration. For example the world seems to be polarized in terms of protection of self interests, equality of opportunity and access to resources. These debates and pressure groups indicate conflict rather than consensus on basic values and goals in society. Second, the concepts of function and dysfunction present problems since what one might consider to be functional within society, somebody else might consider to be dysfunctional or vice versa. Third, Structural-functionalists tend to reify society by considering some things as objects, for example, they often treat education, society, the curriculum as objects. People do not simply respond to an objective pre-determined social system. People on the other hand make and determine meaning to situations and not simply respond to social structure. Fourth, the process of socialization is not a free, automatic and smooth business. Often it is accompanied with coercion to conformity, with some rewards, sanctions and punishment deliberately given. Fifth, the perspective tends to be conservative, judgemental and definitive. It tends to preserve and justify the existing socio culture, the status quo, the traditions, the ethos. In other words, the perspective is attractive to those groups in society in whose interests it is to maintain things as they are. Last, but very crucial is the criticism that structural functionalists tend to emphasize the system, the society with little reference to the individual. Individuals are seen as filling social roles which are required for the perpetuation of the system. Coupled with the reification criticism structural functionalism can be seen as a dehumanizing orientation.

Conflict Perspectives

Conflict theories differ from the functionalist perspective in that they argue that there are fundamental differences of interest between social groups within society. These differences culminate in conflict being a common and persistent aspect of society. So the protagonists of these theories concentrate on the study of the nature, causes, extent, effects and outcomes of conflict. The conflict theory is basically divided into three models, that is, social (classes, layers/strata), economic (interest groups, epochs, means, forces of production), and ideological (ideas, norms, values, apparatuses).

Examples of conflict theories are Marxian (what Karl Marx himself said), Marxism (after Karl Marx), and Weberian (Max Weber). But it must be noted that all these theories, that is functionalism, and conflict perspectives are called the Systems Perspective. They are all interested in studying society as a whole system, at the macro level. That is why they are sometimes referred to as macro theories of society.

Marxian theory of society is so complex that Karl Marx himself, at times got entangled in it. For more information refer to his actual writings like. *De Capital*

This sociological theory became popular and influential during the 1970's for a number of reasons. First, it grew out of the many criticisms of functionalism over its thrust on value consensus. Second, it promised to give answers that the functionalist perspective failed to provide. Third, it was imperative and fashionable to find new areas to explore the dynamic and changing nature of society. The Marxian guru was Karl Marx the German born philosopher, economist and sociologist. The student is encouraged to read as many works by Marxists since there are varied interpretations of the theory. Several schools have developed from his extensive writings. You must also note that Marx wrote in German and what you read are translations and interpretations of what he said. Interpretation of any works is not fact. Hence several schools have evolved and developed from his extensive and complex writings. Suffice to say the Marxian theory attempted to examine society using the following tenets.

Contradiction >< Conflict

The first tenet of Marxian theory is the observation that in order to survive, humans must produce food and material objects. Consequently they enter into social relationships with other people. So production is a social enterprise. The means of production are critical to capitalist production. These are land, buildings, raw materials, and ideas. Production also brings in a technical component called forces of production. Examples are: labour, technology, skills and scientific knowledge used in the process of production. The forces of production and the social relationships of production form the infrastructure of society, that is, the economic basis of society. (Crompton,1993).

The other aspects of society, such as the educational, political, legal institutions, which constitute the *superstructure* are mainly shaped by the infrastructure. A change in the infrastructure would produce a corresponding change in the superstructure.

But, Marx (1867) observed, that all societies contain basic contradictions which involve the exploitation of one social group by another, for example in Capitalist society employers exploit their employees (workers). Here a fundamental conflict of interest is created between social groups since one gains at the expense of another. To ultimately resolve this conflict of interest a struggle ensues. The relations of production also involve the relationship of social groups to the means and forces of production. The means of production include land, raw materials, machinery, buildings, tools. These can legally be owned. *Labour power*, under Capitalism, is not a means of production since the workers are free to sell their labour in return for wages. Contradiction brings in struggle, at times upheavals, and revolutions in an effort to resolve the *dialectical* nature of society. Dialectics can be explained as those principles and situations that subscribe to the law of opposites but are complementary. Examples are: in biology, male and female; in physics, positive and negative; in mathematics, addition and subtraction, multiplication and division; in social sciences, hero and villain; in education, knowledge and ignorance; in religion, good and evil.

So contradiction ushers in change. Major changes in history are a result of new forces of production. *Epochs* (time periods) are born out of new modes of production vis-à-vis new forces of production, for example, Feudal epoch with its ties of lord and vassal. Capitalist epoch with its forces of industrial production: employer and employee. Final epoch of history: Socialist. Communist society would not result from new force of production. It would develop from the resolution of the contradictions in Capitalist society. It would lead to collective ownership, collective production, collective consumption. Ultimately no social group would *exploit* and *oppress* another. An infrastructure without contradiction and conflict would mean the end of history since Communist society would be free of contradictions that generate conflict and change.

Exploitation and Oppression

The conflict of interest between capital and labour, with one group gaining at the expense of the other, would lead to the downfall of Capitalism. According to Marx, only labour produces wealth. The labour power of the workers creates wealth much of which is appropriated by the Capitalists who own the means of production. What is paid to the workers is well below the value of the wealth they produce. This form of exploitation and oppression leads to strife for change. So the role of education, according to Marx, is one of being involved in the struggle to liberate, to free the oppressed and exploited, that is, the workers, the proletariat, from the Capitalists and their allies, the ruling class, the bourgeoisie.

Ideology and Consciousness

Capitalism endeavours to perpetuate its grip and control not only through the infrastructure but through the more subtle, pervasive superstructure. Those who control the infrastructure (land, raw materials, factories), means of production, in fact the economy, shape the superstructure (social, educational, political, legal, religious, mass media apparatuses). Althusser calls these aspects of the superstructure, the ideological apparatus. The apparatus helps to shape the thinking, feelings, desires, aspirations and way of life of people. The dominant social group, or ruling class (the group that owns and controls the means and forces of production) would control the superstructure to protect and further its interests. So beliefs, values, norms etc will reflect and legitimate the relations of production. The dominant ideas, views (ideology) of the dominant class become the ruling class ideology. These ideas justify their power and privilege, and hide from other less privileged members of society the basis of exploitation and oppression on which their dominance rests. Under Capitalism exploitation is disguised by the ideas of *free enterprise, equality, freedom etc.* In reality, all these are illusions. So ideology is a distortion of reality that gives a false picture of society. Even innocent looking religions are used to perpetuate the false consciousness, the illusions, since religion is used to dull people's suffering. Karl Marx said religion is the sigh of the oppressed creature, the sentiment of a heartless world, the soul of soulless conditions…it is indeed the opium of the people.

Because of this false ideology, Marx argues for the people's awakening from this false consciousness as he called on the *workers of the world to unite!* Marx believed that people tended to accept their situations as normal, natural, God given, right and proper. But the contradictions and conflicts of interest inherent in Capitalism, which help to maintain the system, must eventually find expression. This would lead to a revolution that would create a new society with no exploitation and no oppression. When that happens, we would have reached the ultimate goal, that is, scientific socialism, or more appropriately, Communism.

Max Weber (1864 – 1920) also offered a conflict theory to the study of society. Weber believed that the basic units of society were various status groups. Status group membership from this theory is basically derived from three sources. They are, differences in life style based on economic situation, the difference in life situation based on power position, and the differences in life situation deriving directly from socio cultural conditions or institutions. He gave examples of such institutions as geographical origin, ethnicity, religion, education, intellectual or aesthetic socio culture.

So the Weberian theory saw conflict within society as a result of competition between various status groups for the scarce resources that are available in a given society but not simply economic resources. Weber agreed with Marx's analysis of capitalist society but rejected the reliance on the two class conflict, based solely on economic criteria. He argued that in all institutions whether they be political, religious, industrial or educational, there would be considerable conflict between those in authority and those not in authority. Those in authority wield their power through complex bureaucratic organizations and arrangements.

Those sociologists who analyze the social world from the conflict perspective viewed the world as still structured and social life as interrelated institutions. The basic difference with the structural functionalist perspective is that the conflict perspective sees society characterized by flux and change caused by the deliberate action of members, rather than stability. What holds society together is common self- interest and coercion rather than consensus on goals and values. Individuals with similar self- interests group to better pursue those interests, and naturally have to compete with others striving to maximize different self- interests. Available resources are always limited, conflict is seen as a central characteristic of any given society. So some groups' interests must, at some given point in time, dominate at the expense of others.

Thus an element of coercion by the dominant group to have their own way in terms of ideas, allocation of resources, rewards, and even sanctions persists. Inevitably, change results from a temporary solution of the on going conflicts. However, the seeds of continuing conflict are always present as long as different groups are differentially able to satisfy their needs. Conflict theorists find it rather easy to explain social change. If groups in society have different interests and can meet those interests then conflict and coercion remain endemic in society. So change must occur as the groups strive to have their self-interest dominate. Coercion of the less powerful by those with access to power within society, and the threat of potential disintegration of the established order, make change, upheaval and flux endemic.

Criticisms of the Conflict Theory

Though the conflict perspective helps a lot to explain change and flux in societies, it fails to explain how social order could exist solely from coercion of some members to accept the status quo as determined by those with authority. Functionalism would answer this question by saying that the authorities would bring into fold the less fortunate through handouts, benevolent patronage, attempts at socializing them into accepting their positions in life through collective social values.

It has been argued that human life is not all conflict, and that though there is some coercion social stability cannot be enforced. More subtle and effective ways keep society integrated and orderly. Moreover, social critics have suggested that conflict theory proponents are rubble rousers who are inherently radical and disruptive of society.

Conflict theorists insist that change is inherent and endemic, but functionalists would insist that what might be seen as change is just temporary upheaval, social aberration of a transient nature that soon settles back to the established order, though in a modified form. The conflict theorists themselves come from ordered society in terms of education, family, legal systems and so on. Critics see the danger of over emphasizing too few variables in society such as economic determinants, conflict over self-interests. There are other equally important social factors that make society what it is.

The conflict theory has come under heavy criticism from those sociologists who say that since all social systems were human created humans can change them. The human being is a meaning maker instead of just reacting to the economic determinants and the maxim of self-interest. They argue that the nature of society, and the social world, are a result of the interactions of people in various settings and situations.

A summary of the two macro theories helps to bring out the complementary aspects of the perspectives. Horton (1966) summarizes the assumptions about the human being and the nature of society in the consensus and conflict values of society.

He says in the consensus perspective underlies the ideal social positions. The image of a person, and society, is a natural boundary maintaining system of action. The transcendent nature of society, an *entity generis*, is greater than, and different from, the sum of its parts. The lack of transcendence is lack of social control, which means anomy has set in. So there should be positive attitude towards the maintenance of social institutions.

Human nature is seen as *homo duplex*, that is, as half egoistic (self nature), and half altruistic (socialised nature), always in need of restraints for the collective good. At times it is seen as tabula rasa, that is, the person should be equated with the socialisation process. At worst it is seen as *homo damnalus*, that is, it is divided into morally superior and morally inferior persons. Values are viewed as serving the social good, the moving equilibrium, reflecting balance, stability, authority, order, and qualitative growth.

On the conflict perspective Horton says that it views society as a contested struggle between groups with opposed interests, aims and points of view. Human beings constitute society, so society is an extension of people. So the transcendence of society is tantamount to the alienation of the people from their own social nature. Hence, there should be deliberate and positive attitude towards change since change is inevitable.

Human nature is seen as *homo laborans*, that is, existential and an active creator of self and society through practical social action but restrained by the material conditions. Values are viewed as freedom from oppressive systems, reflecting change, action, and qualitative growth to satisfy self-interests.

To sum up the discussion, it is pertinent to point out that no single theory holds the whole truth about people and society. The two macro theories are two of the many faces of the same reality depending on one's point of view. Suffice to say that society should be seen, from the two perspectives, in terms of stability and change, integration and conflict, consensus and coercion.

A look at the micro theories may help further unravel the complexities of human society. Micro theories focus on human interactions, and the human as a meaning maker, and seeker.

Interactionism

The Functionalist Perspective and the Conflict Perspective are also known as *Macro - theories*. Though they provide different theories on society they have a number of factors in common. They take a *holistic* approach in that they examine society as a whole. They also regard society as a system. That is why they are also known as the *Systems theories or the Systems Perspective*. Hence they tend to view human behaviour as a product of the system.

Functionalism regards behaviour as largely directed by norms, values, roles etc. of the social system. Whilst Marxism argues that behaviour is ultimately determined by the economic infrastructure.

On the other hand *interactionism* differs from the macro-theories. Interactionism is sometimes referred to as a *Micro Theory*. It focuses on small-scale, piece-meal actions between individuals. In other words, it concentrates on patterns and processes of interaction by individuals or small groups rather than society as a whole. Interactionism rejects the paramouncy of a social system. Consequently it does not regard human behaviour (*action*) as a response (*reaction*) to the system. As we shall see later, interactionism has a number of sub theories, namely symbolic interactionism, phenomenology and ethnomethodology. At the base of interactionism is the need to communicate effectively with others, to develop rapport with others and flexibility in working with people from a variety of personal orientations, socio cultural and educational backgrounds.

Datta (1984) defines interaction as the basic social process involving the reciprocal communication of facts, ideas, meanings, and resulting in mutual relationships between individuals or groups. The interactionist perspective starts from the premise that *action* is meaningful to those involved. To understand an action requires an *interpretation* of the meaning people give to their actions. So the interactionist theory seeks to understand this process. To understand the action (*act*) it is necessary to discover the meaning held by the *actors*. Meanings are not fixed as they depend on the context of the interaction. Meanings are also created, developed, modified and changed within the process of interaction. So, reality depends on *perceived* meanings, defined situations and *structured* actions.

Construction of Meaning and the Development of Self Concept

Interactionism asserts that *definitions* of situation and self are also of significant concern with the process of interaction and construction of reality. A self-concept develops from interaction processes as a reflection of the reactions of others towards the individual. Actors tend to act in terms of their self concept, for example, if one is defined as responsible, respectable, confident, weak or unintelligent one would tend to see oneself in that light and act accordingly. This *labelling* determines to a large extent one's behaviour.

An individual comes to be defined in certain ways. So an analysis of the way actors interpret the language, gestures, verbal and non-verbal cues, appearance and manner of others would give clues as to how an individual is defined. The individual also defines others using the same cues mentioned above. Example: a learner who is perceived to be dull by teachers and fellow learners may lack confidence and in turn might feel ridiculed, despised and inferior. S/he might perceive the class atmosphere as unfriendly and insecure. A self-fulfilling prophecy may result as the learner develops a poor *self-concept* and hence under achieve.

Negotiation and Role Playing

Interaction processes involve not only definitions of situations, contexts and so on but negotiation occurs for a definition to emerge. Often negotiations reinforce preconceptions. Interactionists, like functionalists, use the concept of role but in a different form. Roles to them are often unclear, ambiguous and vague. So actors have a lot of room to improvise, create, manoeuvre, and negotiate. Consider a new mother, a father with first child; new marriage; and the roles, interactions and negotiations involved. So situations, social contexts are open to negotiation as action proceeds from negotiated meanings that are constructed from interaction.

So socio culture is constantly shifting and changing and no one individual seems to be in control. We are all part of the process though, at given points, some people seem to be more dominant.

Branches of Interactionism

Interactionism has many branches but the theme is basically the same. *Symbolic interactionism* emphasizes the interplay of verbal and non verbal interaction on human behaviour and communication. It sees the organization of social life arising from within the interactions of people within a particular society. Social order is seen as being negotiated amongst the members of society regardless of one's position in society. So through everyday life, society is continuously being organized and reorganized as social arrangements are constantly being worked out. Verbal and non- verbal cues symbolize meaning and construction of reality. The conduct of social affairs can be said to be an intricate ritual of communication control and behavioural exchange. Language and symbols are crucial in the process.

The major concern of symbolic interactionism is to explain how cooperative social behaviour is possible. People are viewed as rational beings who are able to interpret the actions of others, spoken or unspoken, at a given time. People see themselves as others might see them, that is, treating themselves as the object of their own observations.

They are able to take the view of others and see the world, its actions, as they believe others see them. So social order is established and maintained by people's ability to use symbolic behaviour, verbal and non-verbal, to facilitate their interaction and negotiation of meanings in social settings. Thus the social world is viewed as taking on meaning through the defining and interpreting actions of those involved. The symbolic meaning may be stable as meanings developed in past encounters are carried to new encounters provided the settings are the same. But if, and as, settings change new meanings may have to be negotiated and interpreted. Even the same behaviours have new meanings in a different setting.

Phenomenology is sometimes referred to as social phenomenology. It challenges positivists who believe that the methods of the natural sciences can be applied to the study of people. Human beings, and their social behaviour, are seen as phenomena to be studied through what the people themselves do and say. Individuals look at the world through some kind of interpretive framework. Phenomenology is sometimes referred to as an interpretive perspective. Hence, the features of people and society are problematic as they are capable of varied interpretations by individuals. People's behaviour, words and actions do not mean the same thing to everybody at the same point in time.

Symbols do not only have a corporate meaning in society. They also have a contextual (indexical) property that requires sense and meaning making on the part of participants as they interact. Each individual lives, and acts in the world of his/her mind. So phenomenology is concerned with self's experience of self, and the self's experience of other selves and society. So it is all in the mind as people construct their social reality. The emphasis of study should be the essential features of everyday life as experienced by individuals in society. In other words the emphasis and concern are on individual consciousness and the construction of social reality.

Ethnomethodology is an American version of social phenomenology. Ethno-methods, that is, social rules, actions and talk are studied. In other words, ordinary folk or lay methods used by people to make sense of what others do and say are used to study social phenomena. Many things individuals take for granted are also taken for granted by people in similar social contexts. Individuals construct their social reality, generate and maintain their view of the world of concern to the ethnomethodologist.

Criticisms of Interactionist Perspectives

Interactionist perspectives are concerned primarily with how individuals make sense of their interactions in everyday life, in the process constructing their particular reality. But such studies neglect the way in which the individual's position in society might shape the way in which he/she might now construct his/her reality. Phenomenologists claim to go further to examine why it is that individuals come to accept that social reality exists. But such studies usually neglect to take into account the way in which the individual's position in society both at the time of the studied interaction and previously might shape the way in which s/he might now construct reality. The perspective might answer the question on how an individual makes sense of the world but does not answer an equally important question on why the individual constructs reality in one particular way and not another.

Closely related to the above point is the fact that interactionist perspectives neglect the question of power within a particular social interaction. Not all people are equally free to interpret social situations and act upon the interpretations as they would like. When teacher and learner interact the teacher normally has more power and authority to define the situation than the learner. The same is true of the head of an institution when it comes to the teacher.

The other problem with the interactionist perspectives is that they do not account for shifting and changing levels of social consciousness. People's perceptions of others change with time, exposure and deeper knowledge of them.. Love affairs rise and fall as familiarity increases leading to marital bliss or failure. The socio-political and economic highlights and low lights shift with realizations, revelations and failure to deliver on promises given. Examples are rises and falls in popularity polls, opinions and allegiances. Today's angel is tomorrow's devil incarnate. Related to this social phenomenon is the problem of illusions that sustain humans and their social relations. People want to believe in things that sustain them from social agony by alluding to the power of supernatural forces. Beliefs in life-after- earthly life, comfort people's losses of say, loved ones.

Radicalism

The radical perspective is a view that is aimed at a complete change of an existing system. Radicals advocate for an absolute overhaul and refurbishment of a system in particular the education system. They draw for inspiration a lot of ideas from the Marxian and Marxist conflict perspectives. The main proponents of this movement are Ivan Illich, E. Reimer, Paulo Freire, J. Holt, M.W. Njobe, Goodman, J. Kambarage Nyerere. They have written books that advocate radical changes in both education and society. Titles that come to mind are: Deschooling Society (Illich, 1970), School Is Dead (Reimer, 1971), Pedagogy of The Oppressed (Freire, 1972), The Diploma Disease (Dore, 1976), How Children Fail (Holt, 1972), Education For Liberation (Njobe, 1990), Education For Self Reliance (Nyerere, 1965).

The radical perspective is sometimes viewed as an anti-establishment movement for human liberation. It questions the need for the existing socio-economic order, the institutionalization and regimentation of education. Among the chief protagonists of de-schooling society is Ivan Illich. He studied philosophy and religion, not education. He worked and practiced as a catholic priest for some time. Illich laments the institutionalization of education that leads inevitably to mental and physical pollution, social polarization and psychological impotence. The school is viewed as the key mechanism in the perpetuation of decadence and rottenness of modern society. The radicals' salient impression is that curricula and pedagogy compartmentalize learning.

The content of the curriculum is determined by outsiders, with their own agendas, who ignore the learners' interests, socio- culture and socio- economic backgrounds. Schools are seen as repressive institutions which indoctrinate learners, smother creativity and imagination. The education system induces conformity, and stultifies learners into accepting the interests of the powerful. The deschoolers add that the education system is the root cause of the societal problems since schools are regarded as the creators of mindless, conforming and easily manipulated citizenry. Schools select for each successive level those who have at earlier stage of the game, proved themselves good risks for the established order. This means conformity and obedience, therefore, will bring their own rewards. So learners are schooled to confuse teaching with learning, grade advancement with education, and a diploma with competence, which should not be the case.

Radical Solutions

The radicals propose simple yet radical solutions that lie in the abolition of the present education system. They propose that education is about change, so a system oriented by learner needs, flexibility and variety should be put in place. Learners should choose what to learn, when and how to learn. Learners should be left to learn things from their environment incidentally as they interact. Illich advocates skill exchanges in which instructors teach the relevant skills used in daily life to others. These he calls skill centers, not schools. In the same context he proposes learning webs which consist of individuals with similar interests who meet around a problem chosen and defined by their own needs and initiatives. Those who help others to acquire a skill should know how to diagnose learning difficulties and be able to motivate others to learn. The instructor's role becomes that of a consultant, facilitator and auditor. The learner is viewed as an explorer, discoverer and experimenter.

Criticism of the Radical Perspective

While what the radicals say has made people question many of the practices of education and schools there seems to be, for the time being, no substitute for schools as we know them. Schools have been around for too long to be wished away so easily. So the call for an abandonment of the school system as advocated by the radicals is unacceptable to many people, and in particular to most parents. Society at large has got too much respect for schools, and may not imagine itself without them. So society would be comfortable with the reform of the education system to remove many of the concerns of the de-schoolers.

Many people feel uncomfortable with making learners choose what, how and when to learn. So to allow the type of freedom being advocated for by the radicals would result in a state of chaos. Moreover, many people would want to come out of an education system with a record of attendance and achievement in form of grades and certification.

The conflict perspective would regard the radicals as naïve in believing that the education system could change society. They view education as one of the many aspects of the superstructure. It is affected, shaped, controlled and changed by the powerful infrastructure. Those who control the means of production would determine the form, structure and content of education. So if there is to be change in the education system the infrastructure must change first.

The major lesson we get from the study of all these perspectives is that not one single perspective can explain human social behaviour fully. Each one of them attempts to explain some parts of social behaviour better than the other. May be the sum total of their explanations help to explain the myriad of variations and similarities of humanity. A good study, like a good experiment, raises more questions than answers. That is the fascination and excitement of studying sociology.

It is important to note that this chapter is an extension of the previous one. We are attempting here to apply the principles and concepts we have studied in that chapter.

Education can be seen to perform a number of important tasks for society as well as the individual. These would include the passing on of socio cultural values and the training of a future work force. Whatever is said to the contrary, some individuals and social groups are handicapped in the education situation and so under-achieve. Sociologists have suggested, and continue to suggest, a variety of possible explanations pointing to factors in both the home and the school, and also to wider aspects of society. It remains a key question as to how far education can have a positive impact on social, political and economic change and development. Other authorities see the school as distorting socialization by substituting teaching for learning and by encouraging obedience and conformity rather than creativity, innovation and adventure.

A Functionalist Perspective

Durkheim saw the main function of education as the transmission of social norms and values from one generation to the next. So education serves the needs of the social system, contributes to the maintenance of value consensus and social solidarity. Education is used to perpetuate, maintain and reinforce homogeneity by fixing in the child the essential similarities which collective life demands and expects. School rules reflect general societal rules which the child has to learn and respect. Schools provide the vital link between education, the economic and political system through a common curriculum that endeavours to reduce regional or local differences so national standards can be set.

So education tries to impart social, survival and specialized skills in the context of social, economic and political situations. Add to this the value of achievement, success, access to education, status, differential reward for differential achievement, education and selection, role allocation and the functionalist view is almost clear, and complete.

A functionalist analysis comes up with a number of functions that the school performs for society. Among the most significant functions would be what Merton (1975) calls the *manifest* and *latent*, and the *dysfunctional*. The manifest functions are the intended functions that schools aim to fulfill. Examples are:

o   selecting individuals for their future role in society; the school tests abilities in an attempt to ensure that the most suitable and capable people will perform the most important tasks
o   educating the required person power; for literacy, numeracy, and specialized skills are seen as vital to individual and societal development
o   focusing socialization; setting the standards of achievement, values, norms and roles that reflect those of a wider society as discipline and obedience to authority are stressed
o   training children to think logically and critically, through several subject disciplines in the curriculum
o   providing innovators, leaders and the led

Latent functions are those unintended functions that the school and its curricula do not plan for. The *child minding* function of the school has allowed both parents to go out to work. Keeping children away from mischief (off the streets) limits their potential for vandalism and deviance. Transmitting, unwittingly, the hidden curriculum like ethos, linguistic accents, preference for certain type and mode of dress, taste for foods, games and so on.

Dysfunctions refer to those negative effects of an intended and aimed for functions of education vis-à-vis socialization processes, instances are

o   the adverse effects of streaming and too much competition in education can lead to truancy, absenteeism, bunking lessons
o   compensatory behaviour like deviance, aggression, escapism may be as a result of perceived failure, feelings of unhappiness,
o   inferiority complexes such as fear of failure, lack of confidence, poor self-image and so on

A Conflict Perspective

Conflict perspectives on education are based upon the view that groups within existing societies have fundamentally different interests. So education tends to act in the interests of the ruling class in society. It does not matter how education is organized, some people will benefit more than others. Consensus is based on coercion aimed at having the world view of the dominant group accepted as the standard, and norm, for all. Aspects of the superstructure, such as education, the legal system, police, maintain the coercion. Hence, conflict will occur between the dominant class and the under privileged group.

So the major role of education in capitalist societies is the reproduction of labour power. In other words the role of the school is that of fulfilling certain tasks. In this view the school reproduces labour-power to be exploited by training children in the acceptance of and submission to authority, as well as passing on the skills required by that society. The types of schools, the curricula, examinations, tests and measurement are all tailor- made to serve the interests of the ruling class. Education is seen not only as a crucial aspect of the superstructure, but as the main component of the ideological state apparatus. So schools are viewed as part of the indoctrination process of individuals into the values and norms of capitalism or the dominant class. Schools are seen as perpetuating the dominance of the ruling class ideology.

The family, the school, and society are the dominant ideological structures designed to serve the ruling and capitalist class. So the central function of the school is ideological rather than technical. It is to make people accept their place, roles and positions in society, thus legitimating the continuation of an exploitative system. The schools aim at developing certain desirable attitudes so as to respond to social and economic incentives, and to accept hierarchical authority. Schools foster and reinforce the system of social stratification as they legitimize inequalities and the status quo.

So the conflict perspective sees education as a class struggle in which the exploited groups are encouraged to see how the education system, and the society, could be transformed to serve working class and peasant interests. Since social relations in the school are a mirror of those to be found in society, real equality must be inculcated through the proactive mode. Education structures, curricula, measurement and evaluation, school organization should be overhauled to serve the interests of the working and peasant class. The struggle for liberation from the exploitative and oppressive ruling class should find expression in the school. Meritocracy, equal opportunity must give way to egalitarianism and eventually total equality.

An Interactionist Perspective

Interactionists reject the massive generalizations contained in the two perspectives so far outlined. Their interest is on examining the way individuals and groups interact within particular situations in the school. From a limited study that observes behaviour and listens to conversations, it becomes possible to induce generalities about the nature of the school.

The analysis of classroom interaction provides an opportunity to examine the relevance and usefulness of a social phenomenological perspective. A phenomenologist would expect to find significant variations in the stratification processes at work in school and classroom situations. Added to this would be the effects of certain key elements to social interaction. For instance, the effects of material, physical and social environments of the learners and teachers on the learning/ teaching process have a bearing on school and classroom interaction. Both teacher and learner, consciously and subconsciously, create meanings, behaviour, reality and identity. This process is dynamic and open ended.

The interactionist approach examines the way in which the values or prejudices of teachers and other decision makers affect the success or failure of pupils. Different studies by Flanders, Hargreaves, Delamont, Cicourel revealed that teachers, counselors, psychologists based their measurement and evaluation on the basis of their class values and culture; and not on the actual capabilities of the individual children. Rosenthal found that teachers judge learners using class indicators, enhancing the theory of the *self-fulfilling prophecy*. The teachers' attitude and predisposition either led to under achieving or over achieving by learners. Also the self-fulfilling prophecy permeated the class, sex and racial dimensions.

So particular, schools and teachers mirror the attitudes and expectations of society as they tend to label children as capable or less capable. Individuals, of necessity, interact with wider society, and so social attitudes and prejudices become internalized within them.

A Radical Perspective: De-schooling Society

Illich, Reimmer, Holt, Njobe, and Schummacer took a step further from the Marxist perspective, by advocating the radical shift from institutionalizing education to opening it up. The school without walls has been advocated for because schools confuse *teaching* with *learning* and therefore prevent children from realizing their true potential.

The de-schoolers view education as the main vehicle for stratifying learners in society. Social stratification implies the division of society into layers which are distinguished in terms of income and wealth, social status or power; and the role of wealth determining the rest. So de-schoolers reject the narrow goals and the means of attaining them, and instead wish to impose a new set of norms, values and culture. This is similar to the Marxian revolutionary who is motivated by an alternative ideology, the ideology of the school of real life experiences.

De-schoolers propose a simple but radical solution. The answer lies in the abolition of the present system of education. Since schools provide the foundation for all that is to follow, de-schooling lies *at the root of any movement for human liberation.* In place of schools Illich offers two main alternatives

o *Skill Exchanges* in which instructors teach the skills they use in daily life to others. Skills can only be best learned by drills involving systematic instruction.
o *Learning Webs* which consist of individuals with similar interests *who meet around a problem chosen and defined by their own initiative* and who proceed on a basis of *creative and exploratory learning.*

Illich believes that de-schooling would destroy what he calls the *reproductive organ of a consumer society* and lead to the creation of a society in which people can be truly liberated and fulfilled.

Task for Reflection

You may wish to compare and contrast the Marxian view of liberation that involves a revolutionary change in the economic infrastructure of society and the deschooling view, here.

Sociobiology is a research study that endeavours to explain sociological differences and similarities in terms of evolution and natural selection. Natural selection favours traits that spread an individual's genes by increasing the number of the individual's offspring and the number of offspring of close relatives, such as sisters and brothers, who carry many of the same genes. So, biological traits are intertwined with socio-cultural evolution in that as the human species develop they are raised and socialized in groups. Hence, human sociobiology states that socio-cultural traits are selected if they maximize an individual's reproductive success (Lewontin et.al. 1984). Humans tend to forage in a manner that optimizes energy produced, and consumed, per unit of time because it maximizes reproductive success. So most human behaviour is linked to genes investment, that is, the need to reproduce and spread the number of individual offspring.

Human Biogrammars

Sociobiology considers the interaction of genetic and evolutionary factors and how these have been used by sociologists to explain human behavioural similarities and differences. Tiger, and Fox (1972), and Barash (1982) strongly argue that humans behave according to human biogrammar. Biogrammar is a genetically based programme which predisposes humans to behave in certain ways. Though these predispositions can be modified by socio culture, they remain basic influences on human behaviour.

Although the biogrammars of men and women are similar in many ways, there are significant differences between them. Hence, men are more aggressive and dominant. Men are responsible for the protection of the group and for alliances or wars with other groups. That is why and how men monopolize positions of power. On the other hand, women are programmed by their biogrammars to reproduce and care for the children.

Human Change through Natural Selection

In other words, socio biologists believe that humans develop and change through a process of natural selection. (Wilson,.1975). Individuals of a species vary in their physical characteristics and those which are best suited, and adapted, to their environment are most likely to survive and reproduce. Not only do physical characteristics evolve but behaviour also. Behaviour in humans, and other species, is governed by a genetic instruction to maximize the chances of passing on their genes to future generations by breeding. So, male and female humans employ different strategies to maximize their chances of passing on their genes. Human males produce millions of sperm during their life time, whereas females produce only one ovum at a time, and about 400 in their life time. Females also gestate the foetus in their body. Barash (1984) points out that the male has interest in making as many females as possible pregnant to maximize the number of offspring who will carry his genes. The female on the other hand, invests so much time and energy in each offspring that she has to go for quality in her mate. This ensures that each offspring has a good chance of ultimate survival. So she selects only the most genetically suitable male partners.

So the argument goes, that, different reproductive strategies produce different behaviour in males and females. This leads them to occupy different social positions and roles. So males tend to be more promiscuous in sexual behaviour while females are more circumspect in their pursuit of genetic partners. Socio biologists see males and females as simply biologically different, each pursuing the maintenance of their genes in their own way.

Problems and Limitations of Socio biology

However, there are problems and limitations with the socio biologists' claims. Rose, Kamin and Lewontin, (1984) strongly argue that human behaviour is shaped by environment rather than instinct. Unlike most animals, the human infant is born with relatively few of its neural pathways already committed. During its long infancy connections between nerve cells are formed not merely on the basis of specific epigenetic programming but in the light of experience.

Another valid criticism is that socio biologists are ethnocentric. They assume that all human behaviour is the same as that in the 'white' north and western world. Oakley, (1981) points out that there are many societies in the world in which females are more aggressive and less circumspect in selecting mating partners than males. She cites examples of human groups such as the Trobrianders, Lesu, Kurtatchi, Lepcha, Kwoma, Mataco where females take the initiative in sexual relationships. Polyandrous groups reverse the roles taken by polygynous groups. This gives a lie to the socio biologists' attempt to explain universal human behaviour from a western polygynous point of view.

Bleier, (1984) accuses the socio biologists of using selective evidence from the animal world to support their case. She asserts that socio biologists ignore all examples of animal species where males are not aggressive and dominant. She notes that in some species of ape and monkey there are no dominance hierarchies at all. In others, such as the Japanese macaques, the rank of a male within troop depends on the rank of his mother. Recent studies have revealed a wide variety of behaviour patterns in apes. For example some female apes gang up to protect their territory, their food and young from aggressive males.

Then there are those who argue that not all human sexual action results in definite accurate offspring. There are instances of paternity problems in human society, where another male would be the father of the child, not the husband of the wife. Sociologists refer to this possibility by using the saying, 'it is the mother's baby and father's maybe!' This may cause a lot of inheritance disputes in society. However, social convention covers this up by referring to the child's characteristic similarities with some dead forefather…or using expressions like 'an outsider man cannot claim paternity of a child conceived by someone else's legal wife'.

For these, and other, reasons many feminists dismiss sociobiology as a fake attempt to provide selective scientific justification for male domination and power. On the other hand, ecological sociologists see the value of human behaviour analysis that attempts to balance environmental conditions with evolutionary fitness. They contend that humans are neither enslaved to their genes nor divorced from their biology. Social systems are influenced by environmental factors that include type and distribution of food, habitat, seasonal stresses, ecology and selection of mates. Mating systems can be defined by the type of female–male pair bond, that is, monogamy, polygyny, polyandry and promiscuity. The equation is not complete without the genetic factor, of course.

There are also new developments in human endeavour that have affected the laws of natural selection. It may have started with the Mendelian hybridization principles and experimentation. Now we have human interference with bio life. Biotechnology is the science of manipulating living organisms. It covers cloning and the development of genetically modified organisms, among others. These technologies run counter to the basic views of socio biology and its tenets. Biotechnology also has a lot of potential for changing reproduction processes and eventually human sexuality.

Questions for Reflection

What are your views on the claim that we are only humans to a certain extend? Given certain situations like anger, war and xenophobia we revert to our primitive characteristics.

What do you think is the place of human genetic engineering such as human cloning? What do you think of genetically modified organism?

Human courtship and sexual behaviour follow elaborate social rituals based also on genetic make up. Through these rituals and in born characteristics sexual union and reproduction are achieved. Human beings have a number of biologically given needs, such as food, drink, maintenance of certain levels of body temperature and sex. But the ways in which these needs are satisfied or coped with vary widely between, and within, individuals and different socio cultures. While all socio cultures have some form of courtship related to the universal nature of sexual needs, their expression, including the sexual act itself, varies enormously. So the ways in which humans seek to satisfy, or not satisfy, their sexual needs are socio-culturally learned, not genetically implanted.

Reproduction as Production

Reproduction is closely linked to human sexual activity. It is a form of production, the product being new human beings. Reproduction and population growth are controlled through various combinations of socio cultural and natural factors. Socio cultural factors include population regulating practices like artificial fertility controlling mechanisms: pills, condoms, diaphragms, spermicides, abortion drugs and operations. Maltreatment of foetuses, infants and young children is a means of lowering reproduction. These include active attempts to promote foetal deaths (abortion), infant deaths (infanticide). Passive attempts include allowing the infants and young children to die of starvation, drowning, disease or exposure to attack by predators.

Natural factors involve disruption of the menstrual cycle through prolonged lactation (amenorrhea). Prolonged breast-feeding produces the hormone prolactin which regulates mammary activity and inhibits the production of hormones that regulate ovulation. Prolonged nursing can result in birth spacing intervals of three to four years without side effects caused by mechanical and chemical contraceptives. (Short, 1984). Other natural methods that are socio culturally used to regulate fertility are coital abstinence, coitus interruptus (withdrawal before ejaculation), homosexuality, and masturbation.

Costs and Benefits of Rearing Children

The costs and benefits of rearing children are embedded in the process of reproduction. Costs of rearing children start with the birth process itself which is dangerous as it often places the life of the mother at risk. Other costs include the extra food consumed during pregnancy and after birth, the work forgone by the pregnant woman, expenditure on clothing, medical care, education and training. The benefits of reproduction are the genetic investment and the continuation of the species, emotional and sentimental satisfaction from holding and fondling infants, contributions that children make to family up keep, care and socio economic security of parents. Older children contribute to the production of their own food, clothing and housing.

Social Ecological Systems

Ecology is the natural relationship between people, animals and plants and the places (environment) in which they live. Social ecological systems refer to the places, space, or situations in which people with similar interests and circumstances live. The social system includes the domestic sphere of life: dwelling space, shelter, residence, household in which certain universally accepted recurrent activities take place. Although all societies have a domestic sphere of life, there is no single natural way to organize domestic life. There are a number of functions served by domestic organizations such as the family, kinship and marriage. These are sex, reproduction, socialization, subsistence and identity. Domestic activities include preparation and consumption of food, cleaning, grooming, teaching and training the young, sleeping, recreating, and adult sexual intercourse. Much of the social life is organized around the patterns male and female associate. There are three main examples of patterns of male and female association. These are the family, kinship and marriage.

Family Kinships

A family is a group of persons linked by kin connections. Kinship ties are connections between individuals, through marriage or blood relatives. Marriage is a socially acknowledged and approved sexual union between two or more adult individuals. So the family is a kinship group that takes two forms. First, the nuclear family comprises of a husband, wife, and their offspring. Second, the extended family comprises of two or more nuclear families that may include grand parents, brothers, sisters and their spouses, aunts, nephews and cousins.

There are three perennial principal forms of marriage, with the fourth one being of a transient nature. These are monogamy, polygamy, cohabitation and promiscuity. Monogamy is a marriage with one spouse exclusively and possibly for life. Polygamy is marriage with more than one spouse at a time. There are two types of polygamy. Polygyny is marriage in which a man is married to more than one woman at a time. Polyandry is marriage in which a woman is married to more than one man at a time. Cohabitation is a form of marriage in that two, or more, adult people live together in a sexual relationship of some permanence without, strictly speaking, being officially married. Prolonged cohabitation usually leads to the common law wife or husband status. Promiscuity is characterized by the absence of any pair bond between the mates. However, this does not imply a lack of discrimination in selecting a mate. Though there is a high level of selection on varied criteria the association is of a transient nature.

Preferred Marriage Patterns

There are basically two preferential marriage patterns favoured by humans. Human mating patterns exhibit a degree of variation within the two patterns. The two systems are endogyny and exogyny. Endogyny is a system that requires and rules that one has to marry within the group. Exogyny is the system that rules that one has to marry outside the group. The practice is called endogamy and exogamy. Endogamy is the practice that requires an individual to take a spouse from a group or status of which one is a member. So some groups would marry their nephews, cousins, nieces, and even brothers and sisters. Exogamy forbids an individual from taking a spouse from within a prescribed local, kin, status or other group in which they are both members. Incest avoidance and penalties keep such people in check.

The Dark Side of the Domestic Sphere of Life

The domestic sphere of life can be warm, secure and fulfilling but it can be a source of stress and trauma. It can encompass a range of emotionally upsetting experiences. It can be full of tension, violence and traumatized experiences. The domestic atmosphere can be oppressive, conflict ridden and hostile. It can lead to abuse of spouse, and children. The domestic climate can drive people to despair, anxiety, guilt and at times suicide. All this can lead to mental illness, social deviance, and even crime.

Kinship Patterns

There are two basic patterns, or principles involved in kinship organization. People are related through descent or parentage. Descent is the belief that certain persons play an important role in the creation, birth and nurturing of children. Descent could be traced through the father (paternal) or the mother (maternal).

Patrilineality is descent through the male line, and their spouses. The group is headed by a male (patriarch) and is ruled or controlled by men, or female from the father's line (patriarchal). Property is inherited from one's father or father's line (patrimony). The residence is male centred (patrilocal): fathers, brothers, sons form the core of the kinship organization. The prestigious and powerful men form a board of directors of a family style company. They make decisions about the domestic group's holdings in land, livestock, buildings, labour, crops, and fields. They formulate policies and decide on priorities for the group.

Matrilineality is descent through the female line, but not necessarily their spouses. The social group is headed by a female, or male from the mother's line (matriarch), and is ruled or controlled by women (matriarchal). Women own property and have the authority. Their offspring inherit their property (matrimony). The residence is female centred (matrilocal). With matrilocality, mothers, sisters, daughters and aunts form the core of the kinship organization.

Changes in Parenthood

A diversity of family forms exists in societies on the globe. Changes are occurring and creating movements towards single, and double (nuclear) parenting. These have led to the breakdown of the extended family systems and kinship organizations. The directions of change tend to centre on single or one parent families where either a mother or father finds herself or himself raising his offspring single handedly. Many children throughout the world are brought up in domestic groups in which only one parent is present. This may be due to divorce, death, or absence of one of the parents. It may also be due to inability or unwillingness to marry. The most common one parent family has mother only. Such households are called matrifocal. Other reasons may be that the mother has greater access to sources of income than the biological father; the father's access to sources of wealth and income depends on absence from home for extended periods; migration or higher male mortality rates due to disease or warfare leads to shortage of marriage partners.

Multiple Parenting Systems

Multiple parenting systems are socio psychologically friendly, helpful and caring groups with similar expected behaviour, norms and values. These are referred to as avuncular social groups. Extended families and other kinship groups can form multiple parenting groups that share the critical tasks of rearing and bringing up children. In most parts of Africa, Asia and South America children literally belong to the village. Their main benefit is the dispersal of affection effect in times of personal crises like illness, death and hunger. Avuncular groups are declining mainly due to socio and geo economic pressures.

In fact the trend seems to favour no child (nil offspring) families where wife and husband decide not to have any children at all. Again socio and geo economic pressures, diseases such as HIV aids, German measles, and trends and changes in values make couples decide to have no children. Yet parenting principles remain universal in that the young need care. The young need to be provided for in terms of basic needs like water, food, shelter, clothing, basic education, emotional and social security.

Other Causes of Direction of Social change

Other causes of directions of change are varied. Child-led families in Africa are mainly due to the HIV aids pandemic that has killed parents leaving young children in charge of families. The emergence of rises in orphanhood among children is high. Where a child loses a parent, who is the income supporter, is called a single orphan. Where a child loses both parents, is called double orphan. Parents can be lost through death, desertion, or prolonged absence from home. Children's rights could be undermined by having children shouldering responsibilities too early in life.

Socio economic pressures lead many parents to migrate to other countries leaving children to look after themselves creating many problems. Rights of women and female liberation movements have led to free choices of spouse, residence, career by women themselves. So marriages are determined by women rather than by men. The eminence of gay rights has led to gay marriages and gay parent families in which children are brought up by either lesbian partners or two male homosexuals living together. Alternatives to marriages and families are found in communes such as Kibbutz. In extreme cases socio sex satisfaction is catered for in institutions of promiscuity and prostitution. Sex worker groups have taken prominence in western societies in particular, though it should be noted that prostitution is one of the oldest professions in the world.

A novel alternative to the family comes from Toffler (2003). He suggests a system of professional parents. These pro parents would simulate family groups and adopt the roles of father, mother, grant parent, aunt, and uncle. They would train and specialize in child rearing as a paid occupation. He believes this would end the amateur status of child rearing and free the biological parents from their family roles. They would simply hand over their offspring to the professionals.

Feminist Liberation

Women liberation movements range from the liberal to the radical views of family life styles, statuses and roles. The theoretical framework lies in the Marxist views of an egalitarian society. Liberal feminists support a societal system in which there is equality of opportunity and a share of household work and chores between male and female partners. They feel that since male and female have equal abilities this will lead to the gradual disappearance of inequalities between the sexes. They call for modifications to the family with shared roles and collective child rearing. Paradoxically most women in this category say that they are satisfied with, and find fulfillment in marriage. Is this due to the fact that women have been socialized to feel this way?

On the other end radical feminists advocate the abolition of gender roles and the family. Men and women should be seen as people, not as male or female. (Oakley, 1979). Abolishing the family would help break the circle of the daughter learning her role from the mother. Some feminists even suggest androgyny (homosexuality). Firestone (1975)) proposes that babies should be conceived and developed outside the womb. There are even supremacists who believe that women are far superior to men in intelligence, biological fitness and morality. So they foresee women being dominant in a future female paradise.

Questions for Review

What do you see as the place of women in society? Should they play a key role in social, political, religious and economic affairs just as men?

Sociologists discuss ethnic, racial and gender issues in relation to social stratification. Stratification refers to structured inequalities between different groupings of people. Societies consist of strata (layers) in a hierarchy, with the more privileged at the top and the less favoured at the bottom. Stratification has also a lot to do with deviance, discipline and social control.

There are four basic systems of stratification: slavery, caste, estates and class. Slavery is an extreme form of inequality in which some individuals are owned by others as their property. Slaves existed alongside classes in ancient Greece and Rome, and in Europe, and America during the 19th Century. Slavery took on a racial tone when European and Arab slavers commercialized it from the 17th century onwards. West, East and Central Africa suffered most from this form of slavery.

Though slavery in its extreme form has been abolished different forms of slavery persist. Examples are: Cases of human trafficking in which individuals are lured into what seem like lucrative jobs but become social captives for sexual, labour and other forms of work for the benefit of the masters. The feminist movement would argue that many forms of marriage practices especially in Africa and Asia are slavery where women have no say in the process and practice of marriage. Trade and Labour Union movements advocate for the removal of slave wages and adverse conditions of work and employment.

Caste System

The term caste comes from Portuguese *casta* meaning pure stock. It can be used to describe a society that has strict strata with the upper class at the top. This would include the royalty, captains of commerce and industry, celebrities, and the super rich. The second layer would be the middle class. At the lower end would be the working class followed by the under class who have very little material and socio economic resources.

But generally, the caste hierarchy and system are closely bound up with the Hindu belief in rebirth. This does not mean that one must be a Hindu in order to belong to a caste. Muslim and Christian castes exist, especially in India. The basic belief is that people are not spiritually equal so the gods have established a hierarchy of groups. Individuals who fail to abide by the rituals and duties of their caste will be reborn in an inferior position in their next incarnation. This hierarchy consists of the four major *varnas*, or grades of beings, each ranked differently in terms of honour. Those in the highest layer, the Brahmins (priests), represent the most elevated condition of purity, then come the Kshatriyas (warriors), then the Vaishyas (merchants and crafts-persons) and the Shudras (menial workers), the untouchables the lowest. An individual's varna is determined by descent as it corresponds to the varna of one's parents. It cannot be altered during one's lifetime. Each varna has its appropriate rules of behaviour called path of duty, or *dharma*. A dharma is controlled by the practice of certain taboos regarding marriage, eating, and physical proximity. The varna system has also internally stratified subdivisions known as *jatis* (sub castes) that function as endogamous units. The jatis are the social vehicles that convey the caste system.

Estates

Estates were closely connected with feudalism. The feudal estates consisted of strata with differing duties and rights towards each other. In traditional civilizations the highest estate was composed of rulers, aristocracy and gentry. This was followed by the clergy, who enjoyed certain special privileges. Then came the merchants and artisans. Those in the third estate were the commoners: serfs, and free peasants. Unlike in the caste system, a certain degree of inter- marriage and social mobility was tolerated between estates. Commoners could be knighted by the monarch for distinguished service. Merchants might purchase titles. Today we still have this practice in the awards of knighthood, merit honours of valour, courage and vicissitude.

Class

A class is a large scale grouping of people who share common socio economic resources that influence their life style. Ownership of wealth, one's occupation, or lack of them, are the main bases of class differences. Generally there are four major classes. The upper class constitute the wealthy, and those who control and own productive resources. The middle upper class is composed of top executives and captains of commerce and industry. The middle class is composed of professionals, academics and white-collar workers. The working class and peasant class are the lowest in this hierarchy. Sociologists like Wilson call the poorest and lowest people the under class. The concept of class is discussed in this book especially under Marxian and Marxist debate.

Ethnicity

It is important to note that all these systems of social stratification affect people on gender, ethnic and race bases. Ethnicity can be defined as the socio cultural perceptions, conceptions and practices of a given community of people that set them apart from others. Groups within society can be distinguished by language, accent, history, ancestry, religion, styles of dress or adornment, neighbourhood, and skin colour. Ethnic distinctions tend to generate prejudice, discrimination and tensions, mainly due to socio economic inequalities and ethnocentrism. In many parts of the world today struggles between different socio cultural and racial groups are quite common. Some of them do lead to wars. Floods of refugees and immigrants move across frontiers of the world either trying to escape from such conflicts, or in search of a better life. Ethnic group tensions are strongly linked to race. The Jewish holocaust in Europe, the Serb-Bosnian crimes against humanity, the Hutu-Tutsi ethnic cleansing in Ruanda, and the Darfur genocide in Sudan are tragic examples of ethnic intolerance

Race

It is very difficult to come up with a definition of the word race. A number of authorities have mistakenly attempted to put humans into biologically different races. Some have erroneously categorized four or five major races of the world. But humans do not fall into the categories well. Similarities of the human race have made the differences only skin deep. There are no bona fide races, only a range of physical variations in human beings. All human beings inbreed very easily across colours. Human population groups are a genetic continuum. Genetically homo- sapiens sapiens is the same. The genetic diversity within populations that share traits is as varied as the diversity between them. So race is a socially constructed term. Racial differences are physical variations singled out by the members of a community or society as socially significant. Racism is prejudice based on socially significant physical distinctions. So a racist is a person who believes that some individuals are inferior or superior to others as a result of these racial differences.

Racial Pride and Prejudice

Racial prejudice and discrimination have plagued people and nations. Adolf Hitler's belief in the superiority of the German Arian race partly led to the Second World War and its devastating effects. The South African Apartheid system of separation of races, with the Bantu (Africans) at the bottom of the social structure sparked a prolonged struggle for liberation. The Rhodesian White Supremacist class system produced a protracted war of liberation. Though these, and other, wars of liberation led to independence the socio economic and political inequalities have not gone. New classes have emerged and worsened the plight of the low and under classes. The latest Arab spring in North, East Africa and Asia arise from socio economic and political inequalities. The struggle for socio economic and political liberation and freedom continues.

The works of William DuBoi (1933) decry racism all over the world especially in Africa. His vision of the world, and Africa, was loud and clear. He said people of all races are welcome to Africa if they obey its law, seek its needs and interests and love their neighbours as themselves. But the white bigots of the world are solemnly warned that they cannot win. We will be free, we will govern ourselves for our best good. Our wealth and labour belong to us not to thieves at home or abroad. Africa welcomes the world as equals; as masters never. We will fight racism and exploitation forever and curse the blaspheming racists and the heathen liars from hell. Let the white world keep its missionaries at home to teach the golden rule to its corporate thieves. Damn the god of slavery, exploitation and war. Peace on Earth; no more war. The earth of Africa is for its people. Its wealth is for the poor and not for the rich. All Hail Africa! DuBoi, the sociologist, philosopher and Pan Africanist hated and detested racism and exploitation in all their forms.

Gender

The term sex refers to biological and anatomical differences between female and male. So sex refers to physical, or physiological differences of the body. Gender refers to psychological, social and cultural differences between female and males. In other words gender is a result of socio cultural statuses and roles ascribed by society. Socio biologists would argue that there are innate differences of behaviour between males and females. On the other hand there are those who assert that differences in the behaviour of males and females develop through the socio cultural learning of masculinity and femininity. So gender socialization involves the learning of gender roles through social agents such as the family, school, and the media. Attitudes develop stereotyping masculine and feminine tendencies.

Gender as Social Stratification

Many studies on gender have revealed that gender itself is one of the most profound examples of social stratification. Female status carries with it many disadvantages compared with that of males in various areas of social life such as property ownership, employment opportunities, income, domestic work, and so on. Gender ideologies have ingrained roots in humanity. In many socio cultures males believe that they are superior to females not only physically, but socially and mentally. The male knowledge monopoly embraces the belief that males have to control the environment while females look after the domestic sphere. Women are seen as contributing to the four roles of procreating, cooking, cleaning and comforting. Ecclesiastical religions encompass male dominated rituals and myths, and foster male political and religious supremacy. The high priests of Egypt, Mesopotamia, Greece, Rome and ancient Israel, Muslim and Hindu worlds have been men. Males dominated the ecclesiastical organizations of all the world's major religions. Judaism, Islam and Christianity stress the male principle in the formation of the world. They all hold that men were created first, and women second, out of a piece of a man. They identified the creator god as a 'He'. All this runs contrary to the new facts emerging that in the beginning was a woman from the Olduvai Gorge in northern Kenya. The recent archaeological discoveries in East Africa and the DNA tests on them have revealed that all of humanity can be traced to the 'African Eve'.

In spite of calls for female enhancement programmes gender differentiation continues albeit some noble efforts at addressing it. Women are grossly under represented in world power and influential social structures. There are only 10% of women in the judiciary, 9% in senior policing, 6% in political high office, 11% in commercial and industrial enterprises and 15% in scientific and technological fields.

Gender differentiation and stratification are sharpened by the biological set up, and socio-environmental circumstances surrounding the female person. Many socio cultures are witnessing changes in established values about socio sexual behaviour. An important factor must be taken into account here. Young people are reaching physical maturity at an earlier age as a result of improved nutrition, environmental conditions and health care. In mid 19th century Europe, girls generally commenced menstruating at the age of about 17 years. Now the average is around 12 years. (IPPF, 1982). The same process is taking place in the developing world. So adolescents are becoming physically and sexually mature and yet they are still socially, emotionally and psychologically immature.

The Adolescent Problem

So society is faced with problems of early adolescent pregnancy, and possible parenthood. The medical risks are highest for young women of 15 years or below. Reports from most parts of the world suggest that the number of young women seeking abortions is rising rapidly. (WHO, 1982). Research in the city of Benin, Nigeria showed that 61% of women admitted to gynaeocological wards following induced abortion were adolescents, some as young as 12 years old. (IPPF, 1982). Abortion complications in Mama Yemo Hospital in Zaire affected mainly those under 15 years of age. In India, illegal abortions are estimated at 6 million annually, many of them carried out on young, unmarried girls. In the USA two thirds of the one million adolescents who become pregnant choose abortion.

Besides personal distress, socio- psychological trauma, abortion can lead to severe complications, sterility, or even death. In Africa, and Latin America abortion is estimated to be the cause of up to 50% of all maternal deaths. Throughout the world, there is a clear rise in the incidence of sexually transmitted diseases, in particular HIV viral transmission, among adolescents. Early motherhood is a leading cause of ill health and death for young women in developing countries. And those who start their reproductive life early in life tend to face considerable limitations to their educational, social and economic opportunities.

Need For Life education

Many young people today need assistance that would help them to avoid the problems associated with early pregnancy, abortion and sexually transmitted diseases. Traditional systems provided information and guidance on sexuality, reproduction and parenthood. Traditional society supervised courtship, and marriage. There is need to either rebuild or replace them with modern alternatives. Parents and other significant elders should discuss such matters with their children, otherwise the children will have to rely on their peers for their socio sexual knowledge, with disastrous results. School curricula should have a central place for education about socio sexuality. Young people should be discouraged from adopting new patterns of sexual behaviour that have dire consequences.

Information, guidance, and encouragement to develop a personal code of values provide a framework for responsible, mature socio sexual behaviour.

Young people need help to develop into well informed, mature and confident adults who are clear about what they want their lives to be like and are able to plan how to achieve this, for their own benefit and that of others around them. Indeed the quality of life of young people depends on their ability to adjust to change, make informed decisions and actively search for solutions to the problems that confront them. The Egyptian philosopher Seneca advised us that ignorance is invariably more harmful than knowledge: It is better to light a candle than to curse the darkness. Let us light the candle of knowledge in all matters that affect us, and others. We owe it to humanity as a whole!

Deviance, Discipline, and Social control

Deviance, discipline and social control span a wide sociological spectrum. Causes and effects range from socialization, child rearing practices, traumatic experiences to socio cultural variations. They can also be linked to ethnic, racial and gender differentiation. Hence, many explanations and theories have been proffered regarding causes, effects, prevalence and sources of deviance. Social justice systems have evolved in an effort to deal with deviance, discipline and social control. The world is full of violence, intolerance, crime against individuals, groups, women and children.

Deviance can be defined as failure to conform to given norms, mores and values. So it is deviating from set standards of behavior and conduct. It concerns behavior, or actions, which do not conform to the norms, laws and values held by members of the group, or society. Deviance is a relative term, dependant on a group's norms, laws and values. However, there are universal norms, mores and values that a person should conform to, such as those enunciated by the biblical Ten Commandments, the United Nations universal declaration of human rights. Discipline involves measures put in place by social groups to instill good, acceptable conduct and behavior. Social control is the sum total of efforts by social groups to control actions, activities and practices by individuals and groups towards order.

A number of theories have been put forward to explain why people deviate from given norms, mores and values. These range from biological, hereditary, psychological to social theories. There are those who believe that deviant behavior is inborn. It runs in families. Deviants inherit traits towards breaking societal norms, mores and values. Then there are those authorities who speculate that certain individuals' psychological and mental traits lead those particular individuals to deviance. It is in their personality set up.

Sociological theories range from differential association, socialization to social structural strain. Sutherland (1999) argued that certain individuals become deviant through association with significant deviant others. Role models are found in life through violent acts, films, war situations, violent political and religious groups. As children grow up in society they can be socialized into social deviant acts they see, experience and observe. So deviance is learnt. Lermert (1997). Other authorities like Merton (2000) say when there is social structural strain individuals react in different ways. Social strain can be economic, political, ethnic, racial or gender related. He says for most people the tendency is to conform as much as possible. For some it becomes ritualistic, that is, following given rules without questioning. Some individuals would react with self serving innovative strategies. They would seem to be conforming yet devising ways of benefiting from the social structural strain. Yet others would distance themselves from society by having nothing to do with the social group. In other words they retreat from the source of the structural strain. The last, but important group constitutes the rebels. These would actively change the situation for better, even by violent means if need be. They are springs of social upheavals and revolutions.

Deviance is a relative term, dependant on a group's norms, laws and values. It can be a social construct. Therefore, deviant behavior depends on who defines it and on what persons' definition of deviance is. Definers of deviance can be the wealthy and powerful who regard the poor and weak as lazy, untrustworthy, prone to crime and vice. Older people tend to define the young as mischievous, irresponsible and crooked. Men tend to define women as debauched, weak and easily swayed. Ethnic majority tend to regard ethnic minority as uncultured, violent and less human.

Besides the above observations, many authorities believe that deviance is closely linked to social differentiation running along racial, ethnic, gender, religious, political and economic lines. For more detail on deviance and social control read Gwirayi (2010).

Forms of Deviant Groups

Deviance takes many forms. There is deviance of the wealthy. Because they can buy for their sins of commission and omission they seem to get away with their deviant acts. The Zulu have a saying that a rich person's fart does not smell. If anything it should smell good. Deviance of the powerful like political and religious leaders can go unpunished if other powerful groups do not intervene. Because they wield a lot of power and influence they can get away with murder, rape, graft and corruption.

Government deviance can cause a lot of harm to society. Individuals in government can commit acts of deviance because of their positions abusing power and authority. Because they have control of the army, police, prisons and media their deviant activities can be swept under the carpet. Rogue governments are known to commit violence, mass murder and rape on perceived enemies in society. Examples are Adolf Hitler's Germany, Id Amin's Uganda, the Darfur massacres, the Ruanda genocide, the never ending wars in the Congo, the Syrian mass killings in the Middle East. The world is full of blood, violence and refugees. Because of such government deviance the International Court of Justice has been set up to deal with perpetrators of serious human rights violations.

Organized deviance unleashes a lot of human suffering. Drug cartels, contraband peddlers, political cabals, human trafficking groups, terror driven organizations and crime syndicates operate illicit trade, deviant activities as well as illegal actions. Hence, the United Nations agencies, International Police Organization and Amnesty International have to grapple with these deviant groups.

Questions for Reflection

Discuss the place and scope of the International Court of Justice regarding deviant acts by politically, militarily and socially powerful individuals and groups. Should regional and national courts deal with the crimes?

Is national reconciliation and confession enough to atone the crimes and heal the wounds?

Differential education concerns itself with trying to explain why some social groups tend to reach higher levels of educational attainment than others. Differences in achievement and attainment between social groups, classes, males and females, different ethnic groups are examined in the light of the preferred sociological perspective. Various studies have shown that if success is measured in terms of examination passes, the continuation in education to higher levels, attendant employment and social positions in life, then education (schools and teachers) has a lot to answer for the differential success. This chapter will examine explanations of the differences with reference to each type of social group. We will look at the class dimension, sex dimension and racial dimension.

The Social Class Dimension

Research reveals that the higher the social class, the higher the levels of educational success are likely to be. Douglas, Ross and Simpson (1970) found that 50% of lower manual working class pupils of high ability left school early as did 80% of borderline ability pupils, while the figures for the upper middle class were 10% and 20% respectively. The U.K. 1991 *General Household Survey* showed that 51% of the children of professional parents had a degree or other higher education qualification compared to 8% of the children of parents with unskilled manual jobs. Some 60% of the children of parents with unskilled manual jobs had no qualifications, compared to 7% of the children of professional parents.

The Sex Dimension

The U.K. Robbins Report showed that only 25% of university students in the early 1960s were girls, while Douglas, Ross and Simpson (1970) found that at age 15, boys were generally surpassing girls in school performance, except in verbal IQ tests. At primary school level, however, girls have shown greater success than boys in reading, writing and spelling. And more recent studies of O-level results show a closing of the gap between the sexes, with girls enjoying greater success in subjects such as Literature and Biology. A great gap still remains at A-level, especially in Maths and Physics. Seke (1995) found out that girls in Botswana form 1 and 2 classes underachieved because of teacher discrimination in class. Mutubuki (2004) however, discovered that parents, in Mutare urban, would prefer to spend scarce resources on girl children rather than on boy children. This is a new and curious development mainly due to economic benefits accruing from the girl child in adult employment. But many studies have found that girls were expected to attend school up to a certain level, whereas boys would be expected to reach greater educational heights. Parents with girls only, in the family, instead preferred educating boy children of their brothers, sisters, aunts, uncles and so on.

The Racial Dimension

Research undertaken by the Inner London Education Authority, and British National Child Development study have found that *Afro-Caribbean* children of all ages between five and sixteen did less well than their white peers. However, studies by G. Driver have recently suggested that in some schools, West Indian (*black*), and girls in particular, do achieve more success than their *white* counterparts. A study of the Rhodesian O-level results covering 1965 -1979 period show that African schools performed much better than European, Coloured and Asian schools.

There are more explanations of this pattern of differential success. The most obvious explanations for differences in educational achievement and social success are intelligence, genetics, home environment, school environment, the structure and nature of society.

The Intelligence Explanation

Intelligence is usually confused with creativity. Psychologists cover volumes on these terms. Here we should concern ourselves with the social theory of multiple-intelligences (Gardner, and Hatch, 1989). We should, nevertheless, note that intelligence and creativity are sides of the same coin. For where intelligence is called for, creativity is needed.

Intelligence can be viewed as the ability to generate and apply knowledge and skills to general knowledge and domain-specific knowledge areas. Logical mathematical intelligence is seen in the ability to discern logical patterns; and handle long chains of reasoning. Scientists, mathematicians and lawyers come into this category. Linguistic, and musical intelligence shows sensitivity to the use and different functions of language; and appreciation of forms of musical expressiveness. Journalists, poets, composers and musical instrumentalists come into this group. Bodily-kinesthetic intelligence is the ability to control one's body movements and handle objects skillfully. Dancers, jugglers, athletes and gymnasts fall into this category. Spatial intelligence is the capacity to perceive the visual-spatial world accurately and to perform transformations on one's perceptions. Sculptors, engineers, designers, inventors and navigators constitute this group. Interpersonal intelligence is the capacity to discern and respond appropriately to the moods, temperaments, motivations, needs and desires of other people. Therapists, mediators, social theorists, great teachers, preachers and salespersons fall into this category. Intrapersonal intelligence is the ability to know one's own strengths, limitations, and desires for the benefit of self and others. Persons with detailed and accurate self knowledge are the same as those under interpersonal intelligence. All these issues, and persons, have profound impacts on society.

Teaching and learning have to take into account all these multiple intelligence principles since this is the basis of differences in development between countries. Collective intelligence harnesses the varieties of intelligence and creativity to develop all sectors of the economy. Countries that actively work on research and development, networking, consultancy, collective effort and specialization are advanced in technology and scientific expertise. Collective intelligence is the fuel and vehicle of development. The Egyptian, Babylonian and Aztec civilizations flourished on collective intelligence. Countries like Japan, Germany, U.S.A, Britain, Russia and France are advanced because they embrace collective intelligence and creativity to the fullest. On the other hand, Africa's problems of development are linked to lack of use of collective intelligence.

However, the principles of multiple intelligence have been the basis for differential education in many countries. Inter-educational separation (F1, F2 schools in colonial Zimbabwe; grammar, technical or secondary modern schools in the U.K.), and intra-educational separation (streaming, banding) were largely defended on the basis of performance in tests that were based on intelligence. Educational psychologists such as Cyril Burt, Eysenck were influential in the establishment of the above- mentioned systems.

The Genetic Explanation

Eysenk and Jensen have both stressed the role of inherited intelligence in determining educational success and failure. Eysenck said that what children take out of school is directly proportional to what they took in. Jensen has stressed the significance of racial differences in the results of IQ tests. The conclusion of both is that about 80% of intelligence is inherited. On the other hand there are those who say that the environment is paramount. Leon Kamin, Klineberg, reject the relevance of IQ tests by emphasizing the effects of differences on educational experience, physical health, emotional condition, familiarity with the subject matter, knowledge of language, and so on.

The genetic explanation has support in a new finding by geneticists. Latest genetic research has shown that a woman contributes, amongst other things, the intelligence gene and a man the physical characteristics genes. So the intelligence gene comes from the woman, not the man. This explains why a man with more than one wife may find different academic achievement levels between woman A's offspring and woman B's offspring.

The Home Environment

Douglas (1945) found parental income, family size, parental interest, language used in the home (universalistic meanings, or non-logical mode of expressive behaviour) and the home value system (deferred gratification, or rush to earning behaviour) very crucial in determining success or failure. Douglas had studied 5000 children born in the same week in March 1945. Dale and Griffiths (1994) found that parental experience and example were extremely important in determining whether a learner would progress in the secondary school environment. It is well known that the children of families who have suffered severe poverty, in particular material and socio cultural deprivation, seem prone to perpetuate this condition in their own generation. Hence the persistent cycle of deprivation need to be broken. The school and society need to remedy this through proactive and appropriate social policies and programmes.

The School Environment

There is a mismatch between the school socio-culture and that of the home for the majority of learners, especially in Africa. Labov sees the problem of success or failure as being caused by teachers who are neither bilingual nor bicultural, and are therefore unable to understand the pupils they are supposed to be teaching. Rosemary Deem, in Women and Schooling, stresses the role of teachers in reinforcing girls for silence and neatness leading to them not participating in classroom discussions. Ivan Illich argues that the school by its very nature merely leads to a reinforcement of the privileges that already exist in society. He cynically observes that if what we learn at school were all the skills needed to survive as a species we would have long been extinct.

Wider Structure and Nature of Society

The Marxian view is that the role of the school is to maintain existing inequalities in the Capitalist system. Marxists point out that even if equal qualifications are obtained, they mean less in economic opportunity terms to groups already discriminated against in terms of class, sex and race. They argue that existing patterns of inequality cannot be changed by means of the school, but rather require a change in the basic attitudes, practices and beliefs of society. Wealth differences should be eradicated to achieve educational equality of opportunity. The home advantage comes in again with its attendant inequalities. Wealth gives advantage in terms of ability to pay for private or special education; or even attendance of same school may bring in a rich or poor background in terms of books, equipment, access to technology, food resources, clean water, adequate accommodation, parental help and attention. Local control and administration of education can also lead to a continuation of inequalities, e.g., the inability of a relatively poor area to provide educational provisions in the same way as a rich area. So it could, therefore, be argued that the whole administrative ethos, socio-culture, ideology behind the education system require drastic changing.

Questions for Reflection

Should intelligence and social achievement form the basis for choosing a mating partner?

Examine the assertion that poor people have poverty of mind. So it is waste of resources mounting special programs for them.

It is pertinent to give a philosophical overview of the foundations of education so as to put education, justice and social values in perspective. Social values are hinged on the theory of values called axiology. This component of philosophy is critical to the understanding of the basic tenets of education, justice and social values. We will come to it after looking at the philosophical foundations of education, justice and social values.

Approaches to Philosophy

There are three main approaches to philosophy, namely speculative, prescriptive and analytic. Philosophic enquiry is a quest for ultimate understanding, the search for complete truth. Consequently, philosophic enquiry cannot provide definite answers, and is not a cure for all ills. It enquires into our beliefs in a methodical, rational and systematic way. It weighs and balances different points of view and arguments. So philosophy is divided into three main approaches.

Speculative philosophy, speculates, and infers on meaning and order to phenomena, for example, atom, molecule, air, light, universe, mind. It is a way of thinking systematically about all that exists. It is a search for order and wholeness to all knowledge and every experience. It concerns itself with the order or pattern which gives the details their importance and meaning (Akinpelu, 1992). So it is the attempt to find coherence and meaning in the whole realm of thought and experience. It is also an attempt to resolve contradiction.

Prescriptive philosophy seeks to establish rational standards for the assessment and evaluation of values; for the judgment of conduct and for aesthetic appraisal. It examines what is meant by good and bad, by right and wrong, by beautiful and ugly, and by wise and foolish. It asks whether these above mentioned qualities inherent in things, or are projections of our own minds (Barker, 1995). It is the business of prescriptive philosophy to discover, find out, recommend and prescribe principles, guidelines for deciding what actions and qualities most valuable, and to provide rational grounds for their existence: for example constitutions, laws, works of art, contests, music, aims and objectives, religious laws or regulations.

Analytic philosophy concentrates on words and their meanings (semantics): sentences, their construction and the meanings of concepts. It examines notions such as meaning, cause, effect, authority, freedom, equality. It tends to be skeptical and cautious. It tends to be objective, to doubt, to question, to be radical. It often leads to agnosticism, atheism, and a decline in traditional ways and beliefs. It is inclined to experimentation, research, scientific enquiry.

Philosophic Schools of Thought

Philosophic enquiry can also be divided into two major and opposing schools of thought. They are called Idealism and Realism (Materialism). They are sometimes also called branches of philosophy. Idealism describes any philosophic theory which argues that only ideas are real. It argues that what we believe to be external to humanity, that is, what we experience through our senses, does not exist as independent entities. The essence of reality is to be understood in terms of what exists in our minds, spirit or ideas. What exists, what we have, in our minds, the idea itself, is real. We know it exists, it is real because we are directly conscious of it. Whether it has real existence or not we can never be sure. Physical matter, if it exists at all, is dependent upon the existence in, and of, the mind. So knowledge of reality cannot be discovered through empirical enquiry but by revelation, and rational analysis. So, existence, and reality, are governed by supernatural and mystical forces, for example by God. Idealism relates to unreal reality: concepts of god, spiritualism, heaven, supernatural forces, imagination, fantasy, prophesy, sex impulses.

Realism, sometimes called Materialism (Marxist view point), refers to the theory that knowledge received through the senses is true, is a reflection of what really exists. Materialism states that the world of reality consists of real, tangible matter. All this can be discovered by scientific, direct enquiry. It rejects the existence of the mind on its own. Materialism tends to view society, human thought as both contradictory and complementary. Hence, idealism belongs to the conservative and spiritually inclined, and realism cum materialism to the more progressive and scientific. Realism is interested in dialectical materialism, the real practical world of hunger, tears, laughter, the haves, the have- not.

Questions for Reflection

You may wish to look at the following philosophical questions before proceeding reading this chapter: Which of the two major branches of philosophy do you consider to be the more reasonable? Can you give reasoned arguments to support your point of view? Describe two of the three philosophical activities that are of value in the study of the philosophy of education.

Components of Philosophy

Components of philosophy fall into three categories. These go into the formation of a philosophy of education. Metaphysics comes from two words: meta which means above, beyond, behind; physics which is the study of properties of matter, energy. Metaphysics deals with the nature of existence, the nature of a person, and the nature of the world one lives in. It deals with what a person really is, the person's origins, and where the person goes from here. So, the nature of the soul, the spirit, the mind, are examined in the light of their functions. It discusses the existence of God or not, human destiny, predestination, fate, free will, choice and so forth. There are immense implications of metaphysics on religion, education, curriculum, and life in general.

Epistemology is sometimes known as the theory of knowledge. This is the main business of education, that is, imparting knowledge. But what is knowledge, how do you know that you know? The search for knowledge and truth are central to education theory and practice. So epistemology digs into the roots of the knowledge base. Critical questions to an epistemologist are: what do we mean by knowledge? What is to know something? What are the sources of knowledge? How do we know that we know? What knowledge is most worth, is most important? The theory is interested in the problems of knowledge decay, knowledge explosion, knowledge implosion, knowledge limitations. Duncan (1984) in the Encyclopedia of Ignorance marvels at the amount of ignorance that exists in the world, and even among scholars. To him, what we think we know is a drop in the ocean of ignorance!

Types of Knowledge

There are types of knowledge which vary with their methods of acquisition, sources and validation. Revealed knowledge is attributed to come from usually a super human, supernatural source, for example, by the medium of vision, trance. We may wish to refer to religions, prophets, seers, sky gazers, horoscope and palm readers, soothsayers, spirit mediums, Saul and the Damascan vision. This type of knowledge is not open to participant observation, experimentation, replication, nor can it be proven by logic or reasoning. It is based on faith, on belief.

On the other hand inspired knowledge, sometimes referred to as insight knowledge, emanates from the inner mind, the brain being informed by an inert, special, inner sense. This special sense perceives what other people do not perceive. Ordinary occurrences can trigger an insight into new concepts about natural phenomena. Examples are the discoverers of gravitation, atomic structures, energy sources, principles of relativity of objects in the universe. Certain individuals, through out the ages, have come out with insights into phenomena, natural principles, discoveries, inventions that have revolutionized the world. Many of them have made life better and safer for society. Examples are antibiotics, laser energy, electricity, microwave, writing, the alphabet and basic numbers. Some inventions have, however endangered us more, Examples are; atomic and nuclear energy, prime movers that have polluted the earth's atmosphere making it difficult for us to live on planet earth, weapons of mass destruction.

Empirical or scientific knowledge is knowledge that is obtained through observation, through our senses, through personal experience, exploration, experimentation, discovery. The knowledge can be verified for its accuracy, veracity, reliability, validity and truth. It is the basis of scientific enquiry, that is, science. So the scientific method is at the heart of this type of knowledge. It involves itself with endeavouring to unravel natural phenomena such as gravity, energy, matter, forces. Its protagonists vie to unravel causes, effects, consequences and so forth. Scientific inquiry should be rigorous, systematic, replicated, as it investigates phenomena.

Rational knowledge is knowledge derived by reasoning, by inferring new knowledge from what is known already. Given some premise, it can be deduced what follows. The term teacher presupposes a learner; a lawyer, a client; a husband, a wife; preacher, a congregation. So logic, mathematics, statistics, law etcetera depend on reasoning, inferring, deducing. Inductive and deductive reasoning should lead to logical conclusions.

Therefore, it is pertinent to indicate that inspirational knowledge is the mother of empirical knowledge with its, insights, discoveries, inventions, theories and principles. Rational knowledge provides the tools of empirical investigation with its formulae, mathematical equations and calculation, and statistical evidence.

Hence, knowledge, and its bases, is crucial to education since society bases its education system on the types of knowledge it considers most worthy of transmitting, inculcating and fostering, especially in the young and uninitiated. It is the foundation of the school, the curriculum, and the business of teaching and learning.

Axiology, or the Theory of Values, is the third component of philosophy which deals with what values society, people, individuals, education, place on. Values refer to those things, objects, which we need, want, desire, cherish, and appreciate. What is desirable or undesirable, right and wrong, moral and immoral, just and unjust, tolerant and intolerant, charitable and uncharitable, right and privilege, goal, aim, objective, belong to the area of social values. Norms of society are critical to social, political and economic development of people, nation and society at large. Legal frameworks, constitutions, moral and ethical standards, civilized behaviour; all belong to the province of axiology, the theory of values. The theory concerns itself with intellectual, aesthetic, cultural, social, economic, and educational values.

Questions for Reflection

A useful exercise could be to use your knowledge of epistemology so far, to design what you consider to be a balanced menu of primary school subjects. You may want to give detailed reasons for your choice of subjects.

Justice and Social Values

Social norms and values are closely linked to the area of justice and peace. The concept of justice has a lot to do with right and fair behavior, actions, processes and treatment towards others regardless of race, color, class, gender, language, political affiliation, religion or origin. Justice follows the dictum of treating and regarding others as one would wish them do to self. Justice's flipside is human rights actions, processes and behavior. The foundation of the United Nations Charter forms the statute of the International Court of Justice. We will come to this idea later on in the chapter.

A poignant illustration of the processes of social justice is found in the African folklore involving the man, the leopard and the jackal. The leopard had inadvertently got itself into a human made trap. It could not escape from the trap in spite of repeated attempts to do so. Several days later the man came passing by. The leopard pleaded with the man to help it out of the human made trap. The man declined after reminding the leopard of its in born nature to revenge on its perceived enemies. After a long persuasive discussion, the man relented and proceeded to undo the trap.

As soon as the leopard got free it promptly detained the man citing a number of reasons. Firstly, it was the man's fellow human, not a leopard, who had set up the trap in the hope of catching a leopard for its beautiful skin. Secondly, the man was naïve and foolish enough to believe the leopard. Thirdly, in any case the leopard was starving, so there was no way it would allow a god given meal of tender, seasoned human flesh to go. Fourthly, in all honesty did he expect a cat to apologize to a mouse before it consumed its prey? So, as far as the leopard was concerned it was time for the man to pay for the sins of commission, and omission, by his fellow humans. That was retributive justice. Any judge would concur with that. However, the man pleaded with the leopard that they sought adjudication.

First, came the cow. The cow reminded the two of the unjust, unequal and unfair human world. The cow was made to share its calf's milk with humans, young and old. May be this was distributive justice. Second, the cow was made to pull the plough in human fields. It would call that slavery. Third, when the cow became old, it would be killed for meat to be consumed by humans, the bones left for the leopard and hyena. The cow's hide would be used to enslave other cows, including its offspring! What a human world of injustice? So, the cow concluded, it was pay-back time for the man. The leopard agreed totally with the cow. What was good for the cow was good for the man. It asked him whether he needed any further adjudication.

At that point in time the jackal appeared on the scene. It enquired into the cause and source of disagreement between the two. After repeated explanations by the man and the leopard, the jackal said it understood the man was in the trap and it was the leopard which undid the trap to free the man. The leopard became mad with the uncomprehending jackal which could not understand simple explanations. The jackal professed that it could not comprehend issues theoretically. Being a practical animal it needed a repeat of the situation as it were before the man undid the trap. In frustration, and a desire to have its human meal, the leopard jumped into the trap and the man duly locked it up, just as it were before the fact. At this point the jackal asked the man and the leopard for confirmation of the original situation and position. At which the jackal concluded that it was prudent to leave the situation as it were. In the jackal world they called it restorative justice. That was the fairest and quickest way of administering social justice, the jackal told the man.

Forms of Justice

There are four basic forms of justice. These are retributive, distributive, restorative and administrative forms of justice. Retributive justice involves retribution, that is, punishment for wrong doing. In its crude form it is an eye for an eye, an ear for an ear, a limb for a limb. Retributive justice is the commonest form of social justice that is characterized by the presence of judicial officers, police, prisons, gallows and executioners. It is big business in most countries of the world.

Distributive justice involves fair, just and equal distribution of resources to inhabitants of a place, country, region and the world. The functionalist view is that of distributing resources to people on the basis of merit, ability, effort, skill, knowledge and motivation. In short, people should deserve resource allocation. The Marxist view is that people should have equal access to resources and rewards, such as pay, land, water and social services. Society should move towards an egalitarian one. There should be racial, ethnic, gender and class equality of access to resources. On the other hand, the Marxian view is that there should be total equal distribution of means, forces and fruits of production. There should be total equality in terms of resources, products and services.

Restorative justice involves reparation of unfair, unequal and unjust practices, processes and actions regarding human rights, resource allocation and distribution such as land, water, mineral, fishery and forestry resources. Examples abound. Indigenous people have been marginalized and discriminated against by late and new arrivals to an area on earth. In Southern Africa the original occupiers, Khoi Khoin, the San and Congoids were displaced by the Bantu, and later by Europeans, Arabs and Asians. In East Africa the original occupiers the Bantu and Nilotic peoples were marginalized by the Arabs, and Asians, and later by Europeans. In North Africa the Nilotic and Bantu peoples were displaced by the Arabs, Semites and Hamites who came in the 5th Century AD. In Central Africa the Congoids, Bantu and Nilotic were marginalized by new comers to the area. In West Africa the Negroid peoples' land was occupied by Arabs, and later by Europeans. In Europe the indigenous tribes were colonized by Saxons, Vikings, and later by the Romans and Arabs. In Asia the Hamites, Semites and Arabs were occupied by more powerful groups from the Far East and North Europe. In America, the Red Indians, Incas and Aborigines were marginalized by Europeans en masse. In Australasia, the Aborigines and Australoids were displaced by Caucasoids from Europe. So the world is full of peoples who feel that they need restorative justice.

Administrative justice involves fair, just and prompt processing of social justice. It is concerned with fair, quick and efficient application of justice. Justice delayed is justice denied. But there are those who would say that the wheels of justice take time to turn and deliver. Administrative justice also concerns itself with delivery of fair and just remuneration, racial and gender equality, human rights violations and resolution of unjust acts.

Human Rights and Social Justice

Justice's flipside is human rights actions, processes and behavior. On 26 June 1945, the United Nations General Assembly declared solemnly

'We the peoples of the United Nations determined to:

o   save succeeding generations from the scourge of war, which twice in our life time has brought untold sorrow to person-kind,
o   reaffirm faith in fundamental human rights, in the dignity and worth of the human person, [n the equal rights of men and women, and of nations large and small,
o   establish conditions under which justice and the respect for the obligations arising from treaties and other sources of international law can be maintained,
o   promote social progress and better standards of life in larger freedom

And for these ends to

o   practice tolerance and live together in peace with one another as good neighbors,
o   unite our strength to maintain international peace and security and
o   employ international machinery for the promotion of the economic and social advancement of all peoples... '

So, on the United Nation's 60th anniversary, it reaffirmed the universal declaration of human rights, dignity and justice for all! The preamble recognizes the inherent dignity of, the equal and inalienable of all members of the human family as the foundation of freedom, justice and peace in the world. Human beings shall enjoy freedom of speech, belief, and freedom from fear, persecution and want. Whereas, it is essential, if persons are not to be compelled to have recourse, as a last resort, to rebellion against tyranny and oppression, that human rights should be protected by the rule of law. Now therefore, the General Assembly of the United Nations proclaims this universal declaration of human rights as a common standard of achievement of all peoples and all nations. All people and all nations shall strive by example, teaching and education to promote respect for the rights and freedoms, and to secure their universal and effective recognition and observance, among the peoples of member states under their jurisdiction.

Article 1:   All human beings are born free and equal in dignity and rights. They are endowed with reason and conscience, and should act towards one another in a spirit of brother/sisterhood.

Article 2:   Everyone is entitled to all the rights and freedoms set forth in this declaration, without distinction of any kind, such as race, color, sex, language, religion, political or other opinion, national or social origin, property, birth or other status. Furthermore, no distinction shall be made on the basis of political, or jurisdictional or international status of the country or territory to which a person belongs.

Article 3:   Everyone has the right to life, liberty and security of person.

Article 4:   No one shall be held in slavery or servitude; slavery and slave trade shall be prohibited in all their forms.

Article 5:   No one should be subjected to torture or cruel, inhuman or degrading treatment or punishment.

Article 6:   Everyone has the right to recognition everywhere as a person before the law.

Article 7:   All are equal before the law, and are entitled without any discrimination to equal protection of the law'

Article 8:   Everyone has the right to an effective remedy by competent national tribunals for acts violating the fundamental rights granted him/her by the constitution, or by law.

Article 9:   No one shall be subjected to arbitrary arrest, detention or exile.

Article 10:   Everyone is entitled in full equality to a fair and public hearing. Everyone is entitled in full equality to a fair and public hearing by an independent and impartial tribunal, in the determination of his/her rights and obligations, and of any criminal charges against him or her.

Article 11:   Everyone charged with a penal offence has the right to be presumed innocent until proved guilty according to law in a public trial at which he/she had all the guarantees necessary for his/her defence.

Article 12:   No one shall be subjected to arbitrary interference with his/her privacy, family, home, or correspondence, or attacks upon his/her honour and reputation. Everyone has the right to the protection of the law against such interference or attacks.

Article 13:   Everyone has the right to freedom of movement and residence within the borders of each state. Everyone has the right to leave any country, including his/her own, and to return to his/her country.

Article 14:   Everyone has the right to seek, and enjoy, in other countries asylum from persecution. This right may not be invoked in the case of prosecution genuinely arising from non political crimes or from acts contrary to the purposes and principles of the United Nations.

Article 15:   Everyone has the right to a nationality. None shall be arbitrarily deprived of his/her nationality or denied the right to change his/her nationality.

Article 16:   Men and women of full age, without any limitations due to race, nationality, or religion have the right to marry, and to found a family. They are entitled to equal rights as to marriage, during marriage and its dissolution. Marriage shall be entered only with the free and full consent of the intending spouses. The family is the natural and fundamental group unity and is entitled to protection by society and the state.

Article 17:   Everyone has the right to own property alone as well as in association with others. Noone should be arbitrarily deprived of his/her property.

Article 18:   Everyone has the right to freedom of thought, conscience and religion; this right includes freedom to change his/her religion or belief, and freedom, either alone or in community with others and in private or public; to manifest his/her religion or belief in teaching, practice, worship or observance. Everyone has the right to freedom of opinion and expression; this right includes freedom to hold an opinion without interference, and to seek, receive and impart information and ideas through any media and regardless of frontiers.

Article 19: Everyone has the right to freedom of peaceful association and assembly. No one may be compelled to belong to an association.

Article 20: Everyone has the right to take part in the government of his/her country, directly or through freely chosen representatives. Everyone has the right to equal access to public service in his/her country. The will of the people shall be the basis of authority of government, This will shall be expressed in periodic and genuine elections which shall be by universal, equal suffrage, and shall be held by secret vote, or by equivalent pre voting procedures.

Article 21: Everyone, as a member of society, has the right to social security and is entitled to realization, through national effort and international cooperation in accordance with the organization and resources of each state, of the economic, social and cultural rights indispensable for his/her dignity, and free development of his/her personality.

Article 22: Everyone has the right to work, to free choice of employment, to just and favorable conditions of work, and to protection against unemployment. Everyone, without discrimination, has the right to equal pay for equal work. Everyone who works has the right to just and favorable remuneration ensuring for him/herself and his/her family an existence worthy of human dignity, and supplemented if necessary by other means of social protection. Everyone has the right to form and join trade unions for the protection of his/her interests.

Article 23: Everyone has the right to rest and leisure, including reasonable working hours and periodic holidays with pay.

Article 24: Everyone has the right to a standard of living adequate for the health and well being of self, family, including food, clothing, housing, medical care and social services. Everyone has the right to security in the event of unemployment, sickness, disability, widowhood, old age or other lack of livelihood in circumstances beyond one's control. Motherhood and childhood are entitled to special care and assistance. All children, whether born in or out of wedlock, shall enjoy the same social protection.

Article 25: Everyone has the right to education. Education shall be free, at least in the elementary and fundamental stages. Elementary education shall be compulsory. Technical and professional education shall be made generally available, and higher education shall be equally accessible to all on the basis of merit.

Article 26: Education shall be directed to the full development of human intellect and personality, and to the strengthening of respect for human rights and fundamental freedoms. It shall promote understanding, tolerance and friendship among all racial, social and religious groups, nations; and shall further the activities of the United Nations for the maintenance of peace. Parents have the prior right to choose the kind of education that shall be given to their children.

Article 27: Everyone has the right to freely participate in the cultural life of the community, to enjoy the arts, and to share in the scientific advancement and its benefits. Everyone has the right to the protection of the moral and material benefits interests resulting from any scientific, literary or artistic production of which he/she is the author.

Article 28: Everyone is entitled to a social and international order in which the rights and freedoms set forth in this declaration can be fully realized.

Article 29: Everyone has duties to the community in which the free and full development of his/her intellect and personality is possible. In the exercise of his/her rights and freedoms, everyone shall be subject only to such limitations as are determined by law, solely for the underlying principles of securing due recognition and the respect of the rights and freedoms of others, and of meeting the just requirements of morality, public order and general welfare in a democratic society. These rights and freedoms may in no case exercised contrary to the purposes and principles of the United Nations.

Article 30:   Nothing in this declaration may be interpreted as implying for any nation, group or person any right to engage in any activity or to perform any act aimed at the destruction of any of the rights and freedoms set forth herein.

[Source: The United Nations Charter, United Nations, Department of Public Information. New York. NY 10017].

The International Court of Justice

The foundation of the United Nations Charter forms the statute of the International Court of Justice. The court has been instituted in pursuance of protection of human rights and freedoms, promotion of peace and harmony, national and group reconciliation and co-operation. It is involved in the administration of justice in its forms, namely retribution, distribution and restoration. It has two basic branches, the Criminal Court and the Civil Court. The most known is the International Crime Court headquartered at the Hague in the Netherlands. Many a dictator has been tried there for gross violations of human rights such as genocide, murder, wanton rape and torture. Examples are Adolf Hitler's hit men, Augustino Pinoche of Chile, Charles Taylor and his son, Yugoslavia's perpetrators of ethnic cleansing. Many gross human rights violators, especially from Africa are lined up for the International Crime Court, which is an indictment on Africa's poor, and atrocious human rights record. There is very little to be proud of Africa in this area of social life.

Article 92 of the United Nations Charter states that: 'The International Court of Justice shall be the principal judicial organ of the United Nations. It shall function in accordance with the annexed statute, which is based upon the statute of the Permanent Court of International Justice and forms an integral part of the present charter'.

Article 93 states that all members of the United Nations are ipso facto parties to the statutes of the International Court of Justice. Each member of the United Nations undertakes to comply with the decision of the International Court of Justice. If any party to a case fails to perform its obligations incumbent upon it under a judgement by the court, the other party may have recourse to the Security Council which may decide on measures to give effect to the judgement. Other functions of the International Court of Justice include giving advisory opinion on any legal question requested by the Security Council, the General Assembly, or any other organ of the United Nations.

Questions for Discussion

Should the United Nations involve itself with issues affecting individuals and group?

Would national and regional groupings not be able to deal with the issues?

The first, or home, language, sometimes known as the mother tongue, is defined as the language of first contact, and use by a child as it comes into the world. It is the lingua franca, the day-to-day language of communication. So it is the first socio linguistic environment and social construct the child grows up in. It is sometimes referred to as the endoglossic, as opposed to the exoglossic, exposure to language learning and teaching. It is similar to the insider mirror looking image as opposed to the outsider mirror looking image.

The rationale for this chapter stems from the premise that it is the learners' right to learn in their own first, or home, languages. Education in this case is viewed as an empowering process that is hinged on self-esteem, pride, confidence building and motivation. In the end, the product of a sustained education programme is the self - actualization of the individual vis-à-vis the group. Ethnicity, language, socio culture and development are inter-linked. They are also intertwined with inequality, discrimination, under achievement and underdevelopment. Hence, the first language is seen as one of the key areas that can unravel the matrix of social problems emanating from the above areas of concern.

Arguments for Use of First Language in Learning and Teaching

There are compelling arguments for and against the use of first languages in learning and teaching especially in formal education. The first most compelling argument in favour of first language learning and teaching is that these languages face extinction. In other words they could be lost and result in linguistic genocide. Tove Skutnabb-Kangas (2000) argues that first languages are systematically being killed faster than ever. By year 2100, between 90% and 95% of today's 7000 spoken languages may be extinct, or at best, no longer learned by children in their own homes. Tove further warns that the most threatened languages are those spoken by indigenous peoples who are normally marginalized and discriminated against. Most countries are multi-ethnic and multilingual yet certain languages are dominant when it comes to teaching and learning. This is because of the history and practice of education in many developing countries where European and majority group languages make children learn in a language that is not their own. Furthermore, most parents, decision makers and educators prefer education through a dominant, international language such as English, French or Portuguese.

However, some researchers counter-argue that languages die naturally anyway, or metamorphose, as they fail to adapt to a modern technological world which has become a global village. They further claim that indigenous people stand to benefit from more widely spoken and better resourced languages. Moreover, more paying jobs and higher education opportunities are available to speakers of international languages like English and French.

The second argument for learning and teaching in the first language is the loss of data and information needed for survival especially by minority groups. Non degraded ecosystems such as rain forests in the Amazon, Borneo, Papua New Guinea, or arid regions of Southern Africa, are often inhabited by indigenous and traditional peoples. Should their languages disappear, their knowledge and skills about the maintenance of diverse ecosystems and its sustainability also vanish. Important knowledge and skills bases about human survival, that are part of their first languages, disappear too. Tove Skutnabb-Kangas (2000) warns us of the grave dangers that by killing first indigenous languages we are ruining the prerequisites for human life on the planet earth. These prerequisites involve natural disaster risk reduction strategies that protect life and environment on earth, flora and fauna that are crucial to preventive and curative medicine, and the general protection mechanisms involving local environments.

The third argument in support of the use of first language learning and teaching belongs to the United Nations International Convention on the Prevention and Punishment of the Crime of Genocide [E793, 1948]. The formal education of minority children through the medium of a foreign, or dominant, language may lead to linguistic genocide. Article 11(e) defines genocide as 'forcibly transferring children of the group to another group', while article 11(b) defines genocide as 'causing serious bodily or mental harm to members of the group'.

For indigenous people, efforts to revitalize their languages cannot be separated from struggles for democracy, justice and self-determination. Aikman and Kay (2003) say these concerns for minority peoples have led to the 1993 Draft Declaration on the Rights of Indigenous Peoples, which lays out the legal and political demands of indigenous peoples to establish and control education in their own languages. Article 15 specifies that schooling for indigenous and ethnic minority peoples needs to be relevant and recognize the learner's knowledge and languages. Multicultural and multilingual education programmes should be based on understanding peoples' languages in today's national and global societies.

The fourth argument is that first language learning and teaching are cost effective. Pinock (2006) puts up a cost effective argument when she says that policy makers are often reluctant to support first languages as media of instruction on the basis that they are too expensive. Having several languages in one classroom can be very expensive and tricky to handle, the argument goes. Instructors and teachers have to be conversant with the diverse languages, teaching methods and strategies. Learning resources have to be produced and be available. This can be expensive in terms of money, resources, time and space, so the counter argument goes.

On the contrary, a recent review of cost-benefit analyses for the 2006 African Education Ministers' Meeting shows that education programmes starting with the first language and gradually moving into other languages lead to cost savings compared to monolingual programmes. If they are more expensive at the beginning, costs decrease over time and savings far exceed initial investment. The savings can be significant in that first language education (FLE) results in lower drop out rates and repetition rates than traditional approaches where children do not learn in their own languages. Pinock (2006) says that a cost-benefit analysis of FLE programmes shows that they cost more to set up but the costs of moving to FLE are not as high as might be expected. Additional cost-benefits of developing FLE programmes include: scripting and developing local languages for academic and professional use enriches everyone; writing, developing, and publishing textbooks and materials broadens the educational horizon. Developing programmes to train teachers in FLE approaches further staff develops personnel. Better teaching of the dominant language, as a second language, is enhanced through quicker understanding of concepts and ideas.

Pinock further says that moving to an FLE system is estimated to cost just up to 5% of a country's education budget. The time, effort and money spent on retraining teachers benefit the whole education system enriching the country professionally and academically.

Moreover, a multilingual framework of education accommodates every language, socio culture, geo-politics leading to human tolerance, understanding, human dignity and equality. This is the optimum price and benefit that cannot be quantified. All this can ultimately lead to conflict reduction and resolution, and peace in the world.

The fifth argument for FLE resides in the area of the human brain itself. The very young human brain, and mind, can handle 20 or more languages simultaneously without confusion. Some socio linguist researches have put the figure up to 200 over a period of time! So the more languages children learn at a very early age the better for their own development. So the multilingual model, starting with first languages, can enrich the individual, the nation, the region and the world.

Many critics have argued that there is a lopsided emphasis on FLE instead of weighing in with socio economic and production oriented programmes. People, and the world, do not eat, wear, drink and breathe language. If we emphasize the FLE programmes at the expense of the more important socio economic factors we run the grave danger of throwing away the baby with the bath water. Other critics have even asked the basic pedagogical question whether the first language is the key to education for all. Those who argue for FLE have been regarded as indulging in futile actions of flogging a dead horse, or to use an African metaphor, a dead donkey.

I argue here, with support from research and experiences from Africa and the world, granted that all the other factors are relevant and should not be ignored, that language, especially the first language, and communication are equally critical to education and development. Language is the vehicle through which ideas, knowledge and skills on socio economics, geo-politics, culture, education and development are conveyed and transmitted. Poverty and discrimination are the basic causes of inequality. Family status, background, social class, levels of education, and language used are some of the main indicators of developmental and educational attainment. All these factors and other variables are intertwined with early, and later, educational experiences.

So the first language, and multilingual, based education plays a significant role in that it enables access to education in the language in which the child feels most comfortable in increasing significantly that child's chances in life (Dutcher, N. 2003). It is a confidence builder. Hence, FLE has the right of place in education and society, arguing from various points of view. These range from rights-based perspectives, pedagogical cum didactic paradigms to practical action perspectives. So I draw examples, experiences, insights and inspiration from selected world research studies that demonstrate that first language and multilingual education programmes do work successfully.

First language education in Africa

Thanks, and critics would say no thanks, to historical developments in Africa, foreign languages, such as English, French and Portuguese, dominate media of learning and teaching. Hence, language education seldom provides a solid foundation for literacy and numeracy development. Recent studies have shown that instead of learning in a familiar home language, pupils learn through an international language before they know it well enough. A comprehensive study of first language and bilingual education for the Association of Education in Africa (ADEA) and UNESCO's Institute for Education (UIE, 2006) reveals that current systems in Africa show serious flaws.

African countries make young children learn through an international language from grade 1 or within the first 3 to 4 years of primary schooling. The transition from first language (L1) education to learning in the international language (L2) often occurs at the point that learners are expected to jump from reading stories to academic texts. Hassana Alidou et al (2006) noted that learners in Africa need 6 to 8 years of very good second language (L2) before they are ready to use it as a medium of instruction. During this time, strong FLE needs to continue so that learners keep up with the curriculum. The stronger the development of the L1 the stronger the proficiency in the L2.

The ADEU-UIE (2006) study shows that learners do well in early L1 programmes. However, within a year or two of the transition to the international language, achievement slows down and declines to an average of about 30% by the end of secondary schooling. Learners left behind by grade 6 rarely catch up. The system only prepares them for an unsuccessful early exit from school. The research findings also show that L1 literacy development for grades 1 to 3 is valuable but not sufficient. Strong L2 subject teaching for 6 to 8 years is required before L2 can be used as medium of learning and teaching. Premature interruption of L1 education interrupts cognitive and academic development. Low achievement in literacy, mathematics and science is linked to premature use of L2 medium.

Studies in South Africa have shown strong evidence that a first language foundation provides the best platform for learning a second language. Kathleen Heugh (2006) also found out that in South Africa the difference between the national achievement of learners who study through their first language is 69% and that of learners who study through a second language is a mere 32%. So the South African grade 6 achievement by province results have a much higher percentage where the home language is the same as the language of learning and teaching.

Nigeria has about 400 languages to cope with. Though it has a long way to go, in terms of multilingual education, it has taken some bold decisions in that direction. Its education allows for trilingual education in the first language, a national language and English, at primary school level. Only the national languages Hausa, Yoruba and Igbo have widespread use at the primary school level along with English. Learning and teaching materials are being developed in more languages than those mentioned above.

Eritrea seems to have done much better in terms of a multilingual education programme. There are nine national languages in Eritrea. Curricula materials and texts have been developed for eight of the national languages including English. This is a bold decision that endeavours to teach and bridge languages in education.

Tove Skutnabb-Kangas (2000) cites research with indigenous and minority children from all over the world which shows negative results from using a dominant language as the main, or only, teaching language. Examples are many. Canadian Inuit children taught in English reach only grade 4 level after 9 years of schooling. It was found in another research study that English is the greatest barrier to successful classroom learning for Aboriginal children in Australia. Children in first language based bilingual programmes in the USA learn English more rapidly, and do better academically, than those in all-English programmes. Also international research shows that children learn better when they learn through a language they know well.

In the largest ever study of minority education, learners, who reached the highest levels of bilingual and school achievement were those whose first language was the main language of instruction for the longest period of time. Bolivia has one of the largest indigenous populations in Latin America. Nearly 65% of Bolivians belong to one of 34 indigenous groups. Until 1982 children learnt in Spanish as language of teaching and learning. Now Bolivia teaches multilingual and intercultural education. This programme increases self-esteem and makes children happier, more communicative, participative, imaginative and creative. (Albo, 2003). Fourteen indigenous languages, in addition to the major languages Quechua, Aymara and Guarani, alphabets have been standardized and taught successfully in schools.

Bolivian teachers learnt a lot from Peruvian experts in producing and implementing multilingual and intercultural learning and teaching materials. Peruvians had successfully worked on similar programmes in their country. Albo and Amalia (2003) report that a comparison of schools following the new curriculum with traditional primary schools shows that 24% less learners repeat an academic year as opposed to 48%. The level of more than satisfactory educational performance for indigenous children has increased from 19% to 35%.

Albo and Anaya further say that placing indigenous languages at the center of education provides indigenous children with the security and freedom to achieve better results. It also helps maintain their communities' socio cultural values and practices. Using the written form of their own languages gives them a sense of pride and prestige with important implications for participating in national society.

Gender, Language and Inclusion

Discrimination and marginalization of minority groups excludes other vulnerable learners such as girls. For example, when drop out rates rise girls are most affected, be it because of socio economic or schooling in dominant languages. Benson (2005) maintains that new evidence suggests that the inclusive strategies employed in first language-based multilingual education benefit girls even more than boys no matter what group they are from. She says studies in Guinea-Bissau, Mozambique and Niger have found out that more girls enroll in multilingual schools. Girls are also reported to repeat classes less frequently, and stay in school longer than girls learning in the dominant language.

Though Benson concedes that more quantitative and qualitative research that separates data by gender is needed, there are clear indications that girls benefit from learning in their first language due to three main factors. The first factor relates to higher female enrolment. Parents and guardians have more confidence in educational outcomes if their daughters attend a school that communicates in a familiar language with its socio cultural values. Multilingual programmes can convince many traditionalists and caregivers that girls with a formal education could still be good wives, mothers and community members. First language-based schooling also contributes to girls' psychological welfare as they learn better, gain self-esteem, build self-confidence and have higher aspirations for the future, making academic success more achievable (Benson, 2005). So, educational programmes that build on the learners' language, local knowledge, experiences and strengths benefit them, especially girls.

The second factor involves the area of increased parent and community involvement in first language education. FLE encourages families to communicate with teachers, support learners, and to be involved in school decision-making processes. For example, parents of FLE learners in Xai-Xai, Mozambique, get involved in curricula issues, repairing the school premises, and teaching socio cultural matters.

The third factor relates to reduction in exploitation and harassment. Carol Benson (2005) asserts that male teachers from the same linguistic and socio cultural communities as their learners are more subject to social control and values reducing incidences of sexual exploitation and harassment. In Mozambique, for instance, FLE male teachers are called by familial terms such as 'uncle'. These teachers have closer ties with learners' families than teachers who only speak Portuguese.

Bridging Languages in Education: First Language cum Multilingual Education Models

International advocacy for education for all has to encompass the use of first language learning and teaching. For many people in the world schooling is available in languages learners do not fully understand and speak. Concepts and knowledge taught have very little to do with their way of life. Malone (2004) suggests five phases in bridging languages in multilingual education. She justifies this approach on a number of basic learning principles. Learning in one's own language motivates, assimilates knowledge quicker, builds confidence, and enriches one's socio culture. With better didactic principles catered for, drop out rates and failure rates go down significantly.

Malone (2004) suggests a working framework for turning a monolingual system into a multilingual one. This first language-based multilingual education programme acknowledges the right of all learners to education in a language they speak and understand. In this model, learners start school in their home language, and then add an official language, a national language and so on, building fluency and competency for communication and learning. The goals of such programmes cover three basic areas of learning, that is, linguistic competencies, academic competencies and socio-cultural preservation.

The purposes of the first language-based multilingual education encompass five critical policy areas. First, there should be a recognition of all the nation's languages as resources. Second, there must be protection of the personal, socio cultural, geo-political and linguistic rights of everyone including minority peoples. Third, there should be explicit directions regarding the use of first languages as languages of learning and teaching in formal, non-formal and informal education. Fourth, implementation strategies should establish sustained development of reading, writing learning and teaching materials like books, newspapers, texts and literacy schedules. Fifth, guarantees must be put in place for adequate funding of the FLE programmes by governments and aid agencies.

Implications of the Chapter

This chapter has revealed that first language cum multilingual education programmes, from Africa and the world, can be done quite successfully when viewed from the rights-based perspective, from the pedagogical and didactic paradigms and from the practicum framework. So the implications of the chapter are many and varied. Teachers, educators and aid agents could increase awareness of, and commitment to, the significance of language diversity in education. Educators and policy makers can learn from the success stories and adapt them for their own countries. They in turn can sensitize officials, implementers, planners and trainers to the crucial importance of the first language for cognitive and affective development of learners, and the acquisition of additional languages.

National and local authorities should mobilize relevant and sufficient resources for the first language cum multilingual education programmes. Investment in teacher education and training is needed to promote understanding, appreciation, literacy in, and use of, first language cum multilingual education. The establishment of first language cum multilingual education as official state policy should be done through the constitution to ensure that linguistic diversity is reflected in education plans. The nation should protect the socio cultural, political, and linguistic rights of speakers of indigenous languages and their right to education in their own languages. Above all, the need to recognize all the nation's languages as resources, on an equal footing, cannot be emphasized enough.

Possible areas of further research

The chapter, like a good experiment, raises more questions than it answers. So, more research is called for in a number of critical areas. Researchers have to find more, and better, effective ways of convincing doubting Thomases such as policy makers, budget providers and educators to support first language cum multilingual education programmes. More research into scripting, developing curricula materials and appropriate alphabets in local and indigenous languages is necessary. Strategies to measure and evaluate first language cum multilingual education programmes for effectiveness, relevance, reliability, validity, success in transmitting values, customs and mores of indigenous groups should be developed. Researchers should provide implementers with parameters and modalities for establishing, as well as, sustaining first language cum multilingual education models. Studies should be done to develop innovative responses, through action research, to demands, interests and needs in areas of language diversity. Researchers should, as a matter of priority, identify linguistic groups and the language abilities and limitations of children through socio-linguistic mapping and other devices.

A case has been made in this chapter, that indigenous and minority learners should be educated in their own languages with sound teaching and learning of official, dominant, national and international languages. The first language cum multilingual education model is crucial to learning, socialization and development. Education in this perspective is viewed as an empowering process with language as one of the keys to accessing that power. Success in these endeavours should lead to tolerant, equal, understanding and peaceful citizens of a country, a region and the world.

Questions for Review

Should local languages form the basis of school curricula?

Who should determine education policies in a country? Give reasons and specific examples for your answers.

In chapter 4 we have outlined the basic tenets of the main sociological perspectives and how each of these perspectives can provide a different picture of the operations of institutions, systems, functions, processes and events in society. And in chapter 8 we examined why differing sociological perspectives relate to, and affect, views on education. In chapter 9 we observed reasons given by differing sociological schools of thought in explaining differential educational achievement and success in life.

In this chapter we would like to engage in a detailed analysis of specific aspects of education, the social nature of learning, teaching and the classroom. We need to examine the effects and influences of the main actors and players in learning and teaching, that is, the teachers and learners. It is crucial that we take into consideration three basic elements of the social nature of learning and teaching, namely teachers, learners and the curriculum.

Classrooms are places where learning and teaching occur. Learning and teaching involve knowledge, skills, and attitudes. Knowledge of the world is assimilated by individuals in certain ways, as percentages: Practical work and doing are 90% effective; seeing 30% retention is achieved; listening 20% is remembered; and hearing 10% accounts for retention. So, a teacher has to take into account principles of learning such as participation, interest, motivation, remembering and forgetting. Teaching and learning activities should involve doing, viewing, handling, seeing and describing. All the areas of learning, namely, cognitive, affective and aesthetic should be catered for by the teacher. Above all these curricula issues take place within the wider social context of the school, community and society at large.

Most people know something about teaching and learning because they have been involved with teachers one way or the other. Teachers themselves think they know more about the complex nature and problematic activity than what other people perceive it to be. Teachers decide to teach for various reasons. Lortie (1975) identified attractors to teaching as:

> *the interpersonal nature of teaching, the service nature of teaching that provides a valuable service to society, the continuation nature of the occupation, the material benefits of security and steady income, time compatibility nature of teaching with flexible hours and holidays.*

The Socializing Aspects of Teaching and Learning Situations

The socializing aspects of teaching and learning situations tend to make even newly trained teachers teach the way they were taught themselves, especially by teachers they perceived to have been effective teachers. So teachers tend to reaffirm existing practices and relations that have been effective to them rather than seek major changes in school and classroom practices. There are three factors that socialize teachers. These are their own experiences as learners in the school system, their pre-service training as teachers, and the real world of teaching. Classrooms, teaching performance and learning are on going constructions emanating from the nature of the interaction of those involved, that is, teachers, learners, curriculum designers, parents and administrators. The role and effectiveness of the teacher is shaped and judged by the nature of these interactions.

In other words, the teacher's role is shaped by factors within and without the school and classroom contexts. The concept of role can be approached differently depending on the sociological perspective one uses. From the functionalist point of view role is viewed in terms of fitting into expectations that society has made for each position. The role of the teacher is seen in terms of individuals occupying the position of teacher and the learner that of a student. The teacher is expected to pass on, and the learner to receive, the knowledge, skills, values and attitudes that are considered essential to the maintenance of the socio economy and the ideology of society. Teachers are expected to fulfill the role of a teacher in terms of dress, behaviour, personal habits and deportment.

On the one hand, the conflict perspective views the teacher's role as one that is full of constraints from powerful forces and social groups mostly from without the school. What is to be taught, why and how it is taught and learnt comes from examination syllabi, regulations, examining boards and employer requirements. The influence over curricula, of vested interest groups in society affect teachers, content and methodology immensely. Other restraining influences are community expectations, technological innovations, economic changes, learner careers and political changes. So the teacher's role is one of trying to resolve role conflict and inherent contradictions.

On the other hand, the role of the teacher is viewed by interactionists in terms of conscious and unconscious actions meant to create behaviours for certain purposes. Teacher and learner behaviour is shaped by their own backgrounds, objectives, the nature of the interactions between learner and teacher, agendas, meanings and situations. Teacher behaviour is analysed in terms of interaction between self, others and the material and social circumstances of their position.

Whatever perspective is used to analyze the classroom situation, learners also exert tremendous influence on the role of the teacher. Delamont (1984) in Let Battle Commence: Strategies for the Classroom, reveals the underlying social features of classroom interaction. While teachers verbally dominate in class, learners would be quite active in shaping the teacher's behaviour. Teaching progress, and the way the content is taught, is not simply the teacher's decision. They are social decisions negotiated, consciously or subconsciously, by teacher and learner.

Woods (1977) studied classrooms and painted a picture of personal role conflict for teachers brought about by increasing socio-economic and political pressures on their work. Teachers in such situations develop accommodating and survival strategies, usually in collusion with the learners. Through such strategies both teachers and learners avoid major conflicts. Woods (1977) identifies five such strategies:

o   Domination, which is characterized by threats of punishment, command and feigned temper
o   Negotiation, which is summed up by the saying that you play ball with me, and I'll play ball with you
o   Fraternization, which is characterized by identifying with learners in terms of speech, dress; sharing jokes, being comic; indulgence of learner whims at times counter to school rules
o   Ritual and Routine, which is marked by teaching through drills, dictating notes
o   Morale Boosting, which is a way of rationalizing use of less than sound strategies; justifying classroom practices, blaming learners as thugs, thick, dumb idiots

Such strategies and practices do not necessarily facilitate learning. They facilitate survival and become recipe knowledge about teaching and learning in certain types of situations. Recipe knowledge here could be defined as what everyone in the given situation knows and accepts. So the practices of both teacher and learner become legitimated.

Teacher behaviour and teacher-learner interaction afford a very useful framework from which to analyse school and classroom situations. Indeed there are situational and broader societal influences and constraints which cannot be ignored.

The Role of the Teacher

Role refers to a pattern of behaviour associated with, and expected of, people who are filling a given social position. (Hargreaves, 1975). Therefore, the concept indicates a position or status, a pattern of expectations held of an occupant of a position. Roles are interchangeable and are of a diffused nature. With practice and experience role behaviour can become second nature. There are basically two types of role, namely ascribed and achieved roles. We have dealt with this in the previous chapter.

The role of the teacher in the classroom permeates a number of areas. First there is the role of instruction, socialization and evaluation of the learner. This is followed by that of motivating, maintaining control and discipline so as to facilitate learning. Hoyle (1969) gives 14 sub roles of teacher in the classroom. These are: society's representative, judge, resource, helper, referee, detective, object of identification, limiter of anxiety, ego supporter, group leader, parent surrogate, target of hostilities, friend and confidante, object of affection. Some of these roles are contradictory but complementary.

The role of the teacher in the school falls into two dimensions with a number of sub roles linked to them. The first dimension is the teacher's social identity which is viewed through a number of tasks expected of the teacher in the school. These tasks are mediator of learning, disciplinarian, parent substitute, judge, confidante, mediator of society's norms and values interpreter of the curriculum. The second dimension involves the teacher's personal identity. that covers the instrumental and expressive dimensions of teaching and learning. These facilitate the tasks of teaching and learning.

There are also informal roles of the teacher in the school. These informal roles serve 3 basic functions. A teacher is expected to allow for individual self expression by learners. The teacher should allow freedom of expression and opinion in class and in the school. The second function of a teacher's role is to facilitate the efficient working of the school formal organization, including the formal, informal and hidden curricula. The third basic function of the teacher's role is to interpret and modify official goals, aims and procedures to the best of his or her ability.

The role of the teacher also extends to the community. The community expects the teacher to transmit knowledge and skills for the benefit of the community at large. The teacher is also expected to foster the norms, mores, values of the community and society. Socio political pressures can bring their own expectations on the teacher. There may be calls for a teacher in new Africa, or for a people's teacher!

The teacher's role has a lot to do with the status of a teacher in the community and society. Questions have been raised as to whether teaching is a profession or something else. Cynics have said that those who can, do and those who can't, teach. It is useful to look at Hoyle's criteria of a profession. For it to be a profession it must be an essential service. It must have a systematic body of knowledge and verifiable skills base. It should have a lengthy period of academic and practical training, a high degree of autonomy, a code of ethics and in service growth. The teaching profession also has many problems to deal with such as unqualified, under qualified and inexperienced personnel. Foreign and local teachers have different training, backgrounds, expectations, norms and values. In Africa teachers are not as well paid as their counter parts in developed countries. Hence it is not easy to attract people with relevant and better qualifications to the teaching profession. .

The teaching profession has also to contend with problems of accountability in education. There is need to control, monitor, and get feedback on schools' and teachers' activities. There is also need for accountability on monetary, moral and ethical considerations. Schools and teachers test, examine, assess, evaluate, select, classify, promote or even reject learners. Who should be accountable for all these activities of teachers and schools? What roles can be played by parents, learners, government and other stake holders in education?

All these concerns lead to role strain and conflict in education. Hargreaves (1975) defines role conflict as situations in which a social actor experiences difficulty in conforming to the expectations associated with the position he or she occupies. There are many sources of the teacher's role conflict. The nature of the job, and social expectations of the teacher are too many, varied and at times contradictory. This could result in the teacher occupying two or more positions whose roles are incompatible. There is also lack of consensus by stake holders on expectations that make up roles. What compounds the situation is that there are differences between what people say and what they do, teachers included. There is also lack of sufficient preparation for role assigned. At times there is lack of personal qualities on the part of the teacher, or social actor.

Learning and Teaching Styles

Learning and teaching styles are some of the crucial factors in learning. Quality education, methods, content and models subscribe to the rules of styles, hence their significance in this book and education in general.

The term quality refers to the degree and worthiness of a product such as education. Quality also alludes to general and specific excellence of a product offered by an institution. A quality product is judged by its distinctive features, characteristics, attributes and trade marks. It creates bench marks, appeals and sustained choice by its customers. It must be worth of the highest praise: Summa cum laude! It goes beyond magna cum laude. For such an institution and its occupants quality becomes the imperative.

Imperative denotes a thing, an action, that is urgent and essential, demanding immediate attention. It commands attention to itself in an authoritative manner. An imperative goes beyond a motto, beyond a mission statement. Hence, quality commands immediate attention of education providers to deliver on intentions, goals and outcomes. These should be adjudicated through systematic measures of performance, attainment and achievement. These should help steer and direct the institution's curricula, pedagogy and didactics.

The word style attempts to describe quality in the actions and behaviour of an individual, a quality that persists though the content, method and knowledge change. So style is not synonymous with methodology since different people infuse different methods with their own styles. So style is personal. People have different ways of doing things, walking, dancing, eating, playing, learning and teaching. People use different strategies when tackling problems with some strategies more efficient and effective than others.

Learning Styles

A learning, or cognitive, style is an individual's preferred mode of approaching learning tasks and problems based on the learner's point of view. The interplay between personality and learning can be clearly seen in the study of learning styles. Some people are wholists in that they prefer to have the whole picture of a problem or situation before they can tackle the problem or situation. Whilst others prefer to have a series of sub problems or situations to arrive at a solution. Learning, or cognitive style is a relatively new concept in education. Through experience, observation and experimentation a number of useful ideas have evolved.

It is useful to look at two theories, one by the London Open University (1987) and the other by Fisher B.B and Fisher L (1979). The Open University classifies learning styles into two, namely, convergers and divergers. Both categories describe individual's preferred mode of problem solving, thinking or learning. Such preference may be conscious or unconscious and specific to many or only a few tasks.

A converger is regarded as one who tends to be better at finding single correct solutions to problems than at producing many different solutions to problems having no such single solution. Convergers tend to be conservative, single minded and do better in empirical sciences and rational subjects like mathematics. Their world seems to converge on single, correct solutions to problems and situations. A diverger is one who tends to be better at producing many solutions to open ended problems than at solving problems or situations which have a single correct solution. Divergers tend to be open minded and do better in creative arts. Their world seems to diverge bringing in a variety of experiences and multiple solutions to problems and situations. Creativity is the ability to produce original ideas or new solutions to problems and situations.

Fisher B.B and Fisher L (1979) identified ten types of learners with cognitive styles. First is the incremental learner who proceeds in a step by step manner, adding systematically bits and pieces together to gain larger understandings. Larger structures emerge from the meticulous and, at times, tedious adding of piece on piece. Perhaps this type of learner benefits most from programmed learning materials.

The second is the intuitive learner whose cognitive style does not subscribe to traditional logic, chronology, or a step by step sequence. There are leaps and bounds in various directions, sudden insights, and generalizations derived from an unsystematic gathering of information and experiences. The quality of thinking here generally exceeds the learner's verbal ability to describe the steps by which conclusions are reached.

The sensory specialist tends to rely primarily on one sense for the meaningful formation of ideas. While the other senses are intact and functioning, one sense tends to be used. The most commonly identifiable styles are the visual and auditory specialists. The former gains much more from seeing, or reading, about concept to be learned, while the latter needs oral explanations, recording or lectures.

The sensory generalist utilizes almost all the senses in gathering data, and gaining insights. The senses are used not only to gather ideas but to test them against prior knowledge. Closely related to the sensory generalist is the over sensitive learner, who constantly has all antennae out to receive perceptual/ sensory stimuli from all sources. The main tasks of the teacher here are to help block out some stimuli, and to provide settings where selected sensory deprivation is purposely arranged.

The fifth is the emotionally involved learner who is at best in a classroom in which the atmosphere carries a high emotional charge. This learner responds beautifully to the teacher's use of poetry, drama, music and lively descriptions. The favoured method is the active and open discussions. If the teacher touches a raw nerve in these discussions the class witnesses strong disagreement. The teacher has to tread carefully otherwise negative attitudes may develop which may take time to fade away.

The emotionally neutral learner functions best in a learning atmosphere where the emotional tone is low keyed and relatively neutral. Learner tends to be detached, aloof and neutral to emotive debates and discussion. Learner prefers intellectual discussion to emotional discussion.

The seventh is the explicitly structured learner who benefits more when the teacher makes explicit, clear, unambiguous structures for learning. Goals, limits and clear guidelines are essential for both intellectual and behavioural intercourse. The learner feels safe and relaxed in a well defined environment.

The eighth is the open ended structure type of a learner who feels at home and benefits most from an open ended learning environment. The usual parameters of the classroom are recognized but there must be room for divergence, for exploration of relevant yet not explicitly pre planned phenomena.

The ninth is the damaged learner who may be physically normal yet handicapped socio psychologically. The learner's self concept, social competency, aesthetic sensitivity, intellect etc have been damaged in such a manner that s/he develops negative attitudes towards learning. Such a learner adopts coping strategies to avoid learning. Such strategies involve truancy, absenteeism, fantasizing, deviant behavior. This type of learner is easily identifiable since s/he gives teachers learning and disciplinary problems. This type needs special attention and treatment. The last category is the eclectic learner shift who juggles styles and still benefit profitably. This type of learner can use two or more cognitive styles and still benefit from other styles. S/he tends to be an actor playing many parts with ease. This is the ideal learner for the teacher but difficult to come by. Unfortunately for the teacher they are not so common.

It is important to sound several caveats, let the customer beware notices, as regards learning styles. The first is that we must avoid hanging labels on to learners since there are no typical people with the styles discussed above. At most these learning styles are theoretical constructs offered as useful tools for studying, analyzing learning/ teaching situations and processes. The other trap we have to avoid is to associate intelligence, or lack of it, with particular cognitive styles. A good assumption is that high intelligence is useful in any style of learning.

Teaching Styles

Just as learners come in different shapes, sizes, colours and styles, so do teachers. A teaching style is a way of teaching performance depending on the teacher's conception and perception of what his or her role as a teacher. Teaching performance is a systematic organization and presentation of material to be taught depending on the teacher's style. Two teachers can use the same method but differently, and with different styles. So, teaching styles refer to a classroom mode, a pervasive way of approaching the learners that might be consistent with several methods of teaching. (Fisher and Fisher 1979). There is also a close relationship between learning, teaching styles and methods since they are all concerned with learning and teaching. The three are central to the business of learning and teaching.

There are many noticeable teaching styles. Some teachers view their learners as individuals with different backgrounds, experiences, personalities and ways of thinking while others tend to see them as a group with almost the same age, thinking abilities, interests and feelings. Hence teachers vary in their interpretation of their role. The way teachers actually perform in the classroom also differs widely, from the cold aloof character to warm, outgoing and flamboyant type; from the vague and rather lethargic teacher to the energetic, and sometimes, aggressive personality. Hence socio psychologists have come up with many types of teaching styles. These range from the parochial, contradictory, complementary, comical to the parodial.

A more comical but useful description of teacher styles has been put forward by Phelan in Hargreaves (1976). The Socratic style plays on questioning so as to draw out information from learners, never providing answers. The town meeting style concentrates on situations that are ultra democratic with every opinion entertained no matter how trivial. Solutions are arrived at by consensus. The apprenticeship style is dominated by demonstrations as if to say 'Do as I do and you will be a paragon.' The sergeant major style consists of commands, instructions and the insistence on following them to the letter. No deviations are allowed. Threats of retribution are made with zeal. The officer/gentleman/lady style exudes flamboyant, smart and well mannered behaviour. Good manners, order and good character are emphasized. Exhortations to civilized ways of doing things form the main method of teaching. The Sigmund Freud style is clinical in analyzing behaviour, good and bad. The fault does not lie with the learner but with the genetic make up of the individual. Finally the printer's reader style involves writing, printing, reading and meticulous correcting of errors, real or imagined. Copious notes on chalkboard, in note books, hand outs occupy the teaching.

Just as learning styles, some of the teaching styles come in a combination but normally one style tends to dominate. It is also instructing to look at what Fisher and Fisher (1979) have to say about teaching styles. Please note that there are some similarities and overlap with Phelan's description of teaching styles. Fisher and Fisher (1979) provide us with six teacher styles.

The task oriented style has the teacher prescribing materials to be learnt and demanding specific performance from the learners. The tasks to be done are well laid out and performances meticulously recorded. Transgressors are carefully and severely sorted out, and monitored for progress.

The cooperative planner type of teacher plans the means, methods; ends such as aims and goals of instruction. This is done with the cooperation of the learners, guiding them in the required direction. Learners' opinions, participation and involvement are encouraged and, supported and respected.

The learner centred teaching style provides a learner friendly environment based on their needs, interests and views. This style in its pure form is not easy to achieve because of the obvious constraints classrooms, schools and resources impose. What many of such teachers try to do is a balancing act. The teacher tries to have equal concern for all learners and for the content, curricular aims and goals.

The subject centred teacher is preoccupied with transmitting the subject matter. The teacher is obsessed with content, facts and figures. The danger is that the 'covering of the subject' and the focus on organized content may nearly exclude the learner's needs, interests and welfare. Hence, real learning may not take place.

The emotionally exciting style displays the teacher's emotional involvement in teaching. The missionary zeal renders the teaching process high in emotion and excitement. The charged atmosphere may not suit learners with different cognitive styles. This style is the opposite of the emotionally neutral teacher. The teacher endeavours to conduct a learning atmosphere subdued in emotional tone, where rational processes are dominant. Intellectual and logical arguments are encouraged resulting in 'balanced' views.

Concluding Remarks

I have tried to prove that learning, teaching styles and methods are closely interrelated. But we should note that cognitive styles and teaching styles are but theoretical constructs that attempt to describe and reflect on learning and teaching processes. We have seen that styles tend to overlap, but over simplify by parceling out human beings who are not made to fit intellectual constructs. Some learners and teachers shift ground quickly between several styles although one tends to dominate.

In conclusion, it is safe to assume that human beings can change, or rather be made to change. This is the major task of teaching and learning. Hence, learning and teaching styles can be modified and to this end professionals should be prepared to examine, and if need be, to change their teaching styles. Micro teaching techniques could be employed to help effect some of the changes in style. The watch word in this on going transformation towards professional ethics and practice should be change that helps the learner to develop fully.

Questions for Reflection

It may be useful for you to suggest, and justify, ways in which a teacher can resolve the many sources of role conflict. You could also discuss how schools should be held accountable for the education of learners in their care. In what ways can teachers cater for individual learning styles in their learners given constraints like large numbers and finite resources?

At this point it is useful to turn to the other major elements of the teaching learning situation, that is, socio-culture, ideology and knowledge. In other words it is about the sociology of the curriculum.

Chapter 13: Socio-culture, Ideology and Knowledge

The learning teaching situation might appear at first glance as only about choice and arrangement of items of subject matter, apportioning of time on the school time table, and allocating resources for learning. However, these decisions raise fundamental questions about what, and whose, socio-culture is the basis of these decisions. What are the qualities of experience for knowledge and social growth? What type and form of knowledge are decided upon, and by whom? Whose interests and needs are served by the choice of knowledge, subjects and personnel? What external influences determine the learning teaching situation? Educating the young for whom and for what purposes? Hence, moral, ethical, ideological and political issues are raised when curriculum decisions are taken.

Who makes choices about the subjects, subject matter, aims and objectives, in subjects like history, civics, religious and moral education, languages and social studies? Even the informal world of the school raises many serious questions on ideologies being conveyed. Examples are the school rules, the uniform, school assemblies, sports, open days. The class and school organization raises issues of decisions and their motives. Why, and who decides on whether to integrate learners or to segregate them through screening, streaming or banding.

In other words the learning and teaching situation is under tremendous pressure from many interested social, political and economic parties. It is not just neutral subject matter to be learnt but a form of individual, cultural and ideological experience to be shaped and modified as it is transmitted. The medium is both the message and the messenger for overt interest groups. Even literacy and numeracy programmes can be a form of socio political action. So sociologists are keenly interested in examining the functions of education from different points of view. They study areas such as the ideological and political functions of education, the economic and social mobility functions of education, the socio cultural functions of education.

Educational planners and designers claim that the process of education is an intentional transmission of the accumulated forms of knowledge, values and skills. They aim that the curriculum should enable the child to understand the world in its own terms, through its own enquiries. But this may not be true on the ground, in schools and classrooms. In short, the curriculum is about power, social and economic control. Teachers can be useful agents of educational change but they can be great barriers to change and innovation. They have their own points of view, their own perspectives, their own ideologies different from the official perspective. So there could be a big difference between the official and the actual curricula.

The Curriculum

It may be useful at this point to explain the concept and ideas about the curriculum. The curriculum can be defined as the offering of socially valued knowledge, skills and attitudes made available to learners through a variety of arrangements during the time they are at school, college or university. There are four basic elements of the curriculum. First, the curriculum is expected to fulfill certain purposes, usually expressed in form of aims and objectives. Second, All curricula should have the body of material considered educationally worthwhile that is transmitted to the learner. The subject matter containing concepts, ideas and information is called content. Third, All curricula should have methods and strategies to convey and impart the knowledge, skills and content to the learner in the most effective way.. The stated aims and objectives are achieved. Four, there must be assessment and evaluation of the learning outcomes. Evaluation should endeavour to check on whether the aims and objectives have been realized.

Ideology, Educational Values and Indoctrination

It is useful to go back to the ideas of ideology, educational values and indoctrination. Ideology refers to those socio economic, cultural and political processes and practices a society holds true and valuable. Those values would be considered worth passing on from one generation to the next. So the process and practice of education incorporates the whole complex of beliefs, values, knowledge, insights and choices. The critical question is who decides on all these issues, and to what purpose and ends?

Different countries and societies perceive these issues either covertly or overtly. Most western societies would talk of liberal education, conservative values and needs based education. Countries would talk of religious education in terms of Judaic, Christian, Islamic, Hindi, or Buddhist values. State ideologies would talk of conscientization, liberation, self reliance programmes of education. In fact there are so many themes and variations but all couched in ideology and social values. There are many determinants of ideology, values, and direction of education. History, tradition, socio economy, religion, and society are great determinants. The government of the day can determine a lot on society and education, especially in the developing world. Colonial governments dictated the type of school, racially divided system, curricula, school going age, heads, teachers, and so forth. Post colonial governments of the day have also followed suit but for different purposes and ends.

Examples from other Countries

It is instructing to look at some examples of overt ideological systems of education that attempted to actively direct education. Mao Tse-tung's Communist China prescribed and directed ideology in society and education. He blended political and civic education. The learner did not only learn book knowledge but also industrial production, agricultural production, military affairs, work ethics, Mao's socialist consciousness and culture. Education should serve proletarian politics and be combined with productive labour. Every person who received education should develop morally, intellectually and physically. It should enable the learners to temper themselves in the great revolutionary movements of class struggle, the struggle for production and scientific experiment. In the country side schools and colleges should be managed by the poor and peasantry. The emphasis should on combining theory with practice. Education served publicly proclaimed ideological means and ends. For Chairman Mao, knowledge should be used as a means of directing and controlling individual, and group, behaviour towards the promotion of certain value ends.

Another lesson on overt efforts to transform society through education comes from Nyerere's Tanzania. Nyerere (1967) believed that education had, actually or potentially, a powerful formative influence on individuals and society. This is another example of how interest groups try to control the knowledge- content and the value- orientation of the process and product of education, and the curriculum in particular. Those who exercise power and influence construe social class relations and other crucial aspects of social reality. So Nyerere was opposed to an education system that elevated material acquisitiveness and self centredness over initiative and cooperative effort. Education should develop a new value system that espoused anti class tendencies and move towards egalitarian and communitarian ethos. Learners should be encouraged to be flexible and capable of planning their own development. So the curriculum should concentrate on literacy, know ledge, skills and practices that are relevant to society.

Questions for Consideration

Should politicians and ideologues determine educational policy given that the process of education is live politics?

Should the school curriculum be overt, or covert, given the fact that there are active interest groups in society?

One of the essential activities of a sociology student is to relate social issues to the tradition of sociological theory. There are many ways of looking at sociological issues, and many methods of investigation. There are also many ideas on how to deal with these burning issues in society. Societies are complex in nature so sociologists hold different points of view, none of which has a monopoly on wisdom. One should engage in a mental dialogue with one or more of the past, or present towering figures of the discipline. One should take insights from the theory or work of the figure and apply it to one's point of view. Isaac Newton observed that rubbing shoulders with the ideas of great minds makes one reach greater heights of intellectual development. He said

'If I have been able to see further than others, it is because I have stood on the shoulders of intellectual giants!'

Perhaps the best education in the world is that which we acquire from close and distant conversations with intellectual superiors. In learning to know other things and other minds we may become more intimately acquainted with ourselves, and are to ourselves, and others, better worth knowing.

The snapshots of the great figures are also designed to give a human face behind the theories. There are no wrong or right answers to social issues. It depends on a number of factors such as one's point of view, ontological assumptions, preference for a certain theory and own circumstances. What makes these theorists important is that most other sociologists regard their theories as illuminating and applicable to areas of sociological thought.

An important approach to sociological theory looks at the views, and writings, of the great figures of the discipline. There are about 24 figures whose theories are worth examining. But here we will deal with only 12. The towering classical figures are Akhenaton Amenhotep IV, Ibn Khaldun, Auguste Comte, Karl Marx, Emile Durkheim, and Max Weber. They established the main paradigms of the discipline.

1. Akhenaton Amenhotep IV (1375-1358 B.C.)

Akhenaton's full names were Neferkheperura-waenra Ikhnaton. His father was Amenhotep III, the Pharaoh of Egypt. His mother was Tiy, of Negroid blood. His wife was Nefertiti, who was famous for her beauty and charm (Loy, 2001). After the death of his father he became the new powerful ruler of all Egypt and its territories. He had a profound effect on Egypt and the entire world of his day.

Akhenaton was a true, pure revolutionary. Not in the sense of political revolution. It was a revolution that brought complete and drastic change to the social life of the Egyptians. Change never comes easily. Yet change is inevitable and necessary for life and survival. Change makes life worth living and is the essence of social history. In this sense social history is the story of revolutionaries.

Akhenaton produced a revolution that symbolized ideas, hope, promise and a better life for all. (Rempel, 2004). Thirteen hundred years before Moses' Judaism, and later Jesus Christ, Akhenaton preached and lived a gospel of perfect love, brotherhood, good neighbourliness, and earthly truth. Two thousand years before Mohammed, he taught the doctrine of the One God. Three thousand years before Charles Darwin, he sensed the unity that runs through all living things. With his wife Nefertiti, they personified love and devotion to family life of beautiful daughters. The relationship between Akhenaton and Nefertiti was one of social history's first well known love stories of song, dance and drama, some of it in written form. At the prompting of the two lovers, the artists and sculptors began to recreate life in its natural state, instead of the rigid and lifeless forms of the then Egyptian art. (True, 2002).

The Dozen Cardinal Points of Life: Leaving a Legacy

Akhenaton and his wife taught the cardinal points where life was to be utilized to the fullest by going beyond self actualization to reach the transcending stage. This was the stage of leaving a permanent record of one's perfect work, a legacy for the offspring, neighbours, society and the world. The dozen cardinal points of life were part of the curriculum, social values and norms of Egyptian civilization:

1. Love all people, creatures, great or small. For you don't know what you are!
2. Invest in people; make friends, connect with people of ideas; always want to learn, share and compare notes
3. Never call people, your enemies. They are simply in opposition, with opposing views. Note today's so called enemy could be tomorrow's close associate. Always address people as my friend, regardless of differences

4. Avoid revenge, hatred, negative feelings. They take a lot of energy, time and effort with no positive returns. Instead work on your own development, projects and success

5. Never think you can cheat other people. You may cheat some for some time but not for all time. The lies, like chickens, will come home to roost. You can't be smarter, cleverer than other people

6. Speak no evil, preach love. It is a great virtue, a noble thing

7. Be honest with people, and yourself. Remember for wrong things, and evil, to continue, good, honest people keep quiet

8. Speak, practise and work for justice, fair play and equality; all people yearn for them, including you!

9. Speak and strive for peace, comfort of others, tolerance, fairness. Note today's safe person can be tomorrow's refugee, today's president can be tomorrow's prisoner…today's executioner, tormentor, persecutor is tomorrow's victim

10. Don't rush through life as if you, or your house, are on fire. Relax, have time for others. A smile does wonders for me and you!

11. Above all remember no one is larger than life. You will not come out of life alive any way. No one, even you, is indispensable

12. Remember to leave a legacy of investment, comfort, love, harmony, generosity, environmental conservation for your offspring, neighbours, and people of the world!

The Blossoming of a New Socio Culture

The blossoming of a new culture signified the end of the ancient socio culture of many gods. Life had then revolved around the river Nile, its soil and the sun. Hence, the Egyptians had worshiped the 4 gods: The one supreme god was Ra, the supreme cosmic power. More closely involved in the Egyptian daily life were Osiris, Isis and Horus. That trinity had to do with the vital forces of the Nile and its banks. Osiris represented the fertilizing power of the Nile. Isis stood for the reproductive earth and Horus the vital force in the vegetation, which was the fruit of the union of the first two. This naturally involved an annual rhythm. So social life then centred on celebrating the vital forces of the 3 gods, and ultimately Ra, the solar supreme power above. The pharaoh presided over all these religious and social ceremonies to the satisfaction of all, the gods included. The totality of the gods were then called Amon. So Amon had to be satisfied with all the rituals.

That was what Akhenaton dared to change with universal success in a comparatively short time. His methodology for change was by decree, exhortation, example and enthusiasm. The new king changed his name from Amenhotep (Amon is satisfied) to Akhenaton (Aton is satisfied). Erasures on temples, literature, and monuments of gods and Amon were made with immediate effect. Only one almighty all powerful God, Aton, was promulgated. The all powerful God nd message were spread to all the corners of Egypt, Nubia in Sudan, and Syria. The new faith, the gospel, in God with limitless power, was propagated and practiced by all humanity, and the known world. (Mutubuki, 2004). This was a God of love, fairness, social justice and peace in the world. Hence, he stopped all expansionism, imperialism and aggression. People were to be involved in productive work, harmonious relations, cooperation with celebrations through worship of one God, Aton.

A Revolution in a Short Space of Time

It is important to note that all these revolutionary changes took place in just 15 years of his rule. Akhenaton's social revolution affected all aspects of life. He established a world of things as they were, in wholesome naturalness. All this cut across tradition and custom. Naturally all that produced resistance to change. The old order had been erased all of a sudden. Priests of the old order who had benefited from offerings and rituals lost their jobs and income. Bakers no longer made a living from the sale of ceremonial cakes at the temple feasts and festivals. Craftsmen no longer sold their trinkets at temple gates. Sculptors and tombstone makers went bankrupt. Magicians no longer collected money and goods for expelling evil spirits. And solders, commanders and field marshals no longer went to new lands to conquer, plunder and loot (Rempel, 2006). Like in all revolutions the greatest barrier to change came from entrenched religious and political power structures.

A Social Theorist and Practitioner

Arguably, Akhenaton is viewed as a social theorist and practitioner who took advantage of his position as king to change the world, transform its thinking, and produce a different but progressive world view. He was a philosopher king who departed from war and expansionism, and moved to world order and peace. He loathed authoritarian rule. He observed that autocrats were not endowed with intelligence but with cunningness. Hence, their demise would be inevitable in the short and long term. His famous saying warned dictators that the ear that does not listen accompanies the head that is cut off. If people say no to one's authority, power and leadership, then one should let go and relinquish office. With that dictum in mind and practice one would not go wrong in social human relations.

His views on one supreme God of the universe, has influenced monotheism in Judaism, Christianity and Islam. In the process he erased belief in many gods, that is, polytheism. He combined intellectual prowess with love of humanity and peace. He was a man who was ahead of his time. He was an intellectual and social leader of tomorrow. He was the world's first true revolutionary who fully believed in, and practised, his social theory so that all of society would eventually benefit by it.

His views on education were that universal basic education was meant to produce citizens who were literate in all areas of basic knowledge and skills. The second level of education concerned itself with developing mastery of mathematical, scientific and technical knowledge. Selected students went through the second level of education. Functional artisans and technicians came out to build the pyramids, sphinx, irrigation systems and monuments. They would do all these under the guidance and supervision of scientists, engineers, architects and specialists from the tertiary level, that is, the grand lodges. Highly selected students attended the tertiary schools called grand lodges, equivalent to universities today. In ancient Egypt they were three, namely, Heliopolis, Luxor and Sais. Heliopolis majored in leadership, healing, religion and miracles. Its famous students were Moshe, and much later Jesus of Nazareth. Luxor concentrated on medicine and music. Its famous student was Zipporah, who later on married Moshe. Sais specialized in cosmics, earth sciences, technology and agriculture. (Mutubuki, 2003). The theme that ran through the grand lodges' curriculum was the sharpening, honing and polishing of the intellect, mind and personality of the learner. That was the business of tertiary and higher education. Any society devoid of the intellectual personnel would inevitably suffer drought and bankruptcy of leadership, ideas, innovation and initiative.

2. Khaldun, Ibn (1332- ?)

Ibn Khaldun was born in Tunis, North Africa, in 1332. He is one of the earliest scholars to use the social historical approach to the study of society and social life. (Bloom and Ottong 1987). He wrote his book called The Muqaddimah, The Universal Truth, in 1370. It is significant that more than 600 years ago a scholar of African origin was trying to understand society by observing the realities of its social past and its present complexities.

His first point of departure was the use of the concept of matter to study its use and application to solving problems affecting social life and development. He explained matter as those natural things constituting matter like solids, liquids and gases. He observed that solids like rock, soil, minerals would be essential in construction, agriculture and industry. Liquids such as water would be used for agriculture, drinking, industry and transportation. Gases like air, oxygen, nitrogen and hydrogen would be used in health, industry and agriculture. When matter was utilized in conjunction with natural forms of energy it opened up a whole range of scientific discoveries, inventions and possibilities. Examples of natural forms of energy would be light, heat, wind, wave, potential and kinetic energy, electronic, electrical and chemical energy. Matter and energy in the minds and hands of intelligent and creative individuals in a group would lead to a better life for all. Civilizations would thrive on matter and energy vis-a-vis active minds in society. This would also lead to collective intelligence and creativity where groups and associations of persons with same needs and interests would further enrich the utilization of the principles inherent in natural forms of matter and energy. All this would produce basic machines such as the wheel and axle, moments and lever, wedge, the inclined plane which would revolutionize industry, commerce, agriculture, construction and transportation.

To Khaldun, it was the prudent and efficient utilization of matter, energy and machines in their many forms that determined the quality and quantity of human social life. Hence, civilizations grew among human groups that efficiently, prudently, intelligently and creatively applied the principles inherent in matter, energy and basic machines. So, education grew out of sedentary life which naturally led to formal education, which in turn, was used to teach, learn, train and cultivate skills, knowledge, norms and values peculiar to the needs, interests and wants of particular human groups.

His second point of departure was the analysis of the nature of human civilization in general. He compared conditions of life in different types of civilization with different forms of government.

Contrasting Sedentary and Nomadic Life Styles

He went further to contrast the ways of life of sedentary and nomadic lives. By sedentary life Ibn meant settled urban communities. By nomadic life he referred to wandering communities. He studied how these wandering groups eventually became settled, urban and wealthier. In other words Ibn was interested in the evolution, and social change, of the states of his time. He observed a century long cycle from nomadic to wealthy urban, to corrupt and decaying urban. (Bloom and Ottong, 1987).

In short, here was a scholar who produced a classic account of the rise and fall of civilizations, mainly due to human social failings of greed, selfishness, corruption and vanity. Ibn put a scholarly finger on what has been, and continues to be, the fate and destiny of civilizations, and nation states. He observed that social uprisings had butterfly effects on other nation states in the region. Revolutions tended to have roots in leadership failure. One cannot help but recall Shakespeare's admonition that the fate of humans lies not in their stars but in social human failings. .

3. Auguste Comte (1798-1857)

He was a French man who had studied the natural science of physics. As a physicist he believed in empirical evidence. So, social life, people and society had to be studied just as rigorously as the scientific world. To arrive at the truth scientific rigour and methods had to be utilized. So he called the study of social life social physics. . He later on changed it to sociology. He postulated that the new field of sociology would lead to better understanding of social life with its social facts.

He ranked sociology as a natural science in the footsteps of biology, chemistry and physics. He strongly felt that human beings were different from animals since they were driven by social facts. So Auguste Comte is reputed to be the first theorist to call the discipline, sociology.

Three Stages of Social Evolution

Comte believed that humanity has evolved through 3 stages. In the first stage humans had tried to understand their world in supernatural terms. Magical and religious forces have been perceived to control their lives. Humans were seen to be defenceless in coping with problems of the real world. Myths and mysteries governed their lives. (Bloom and Ottong, 1987). In the second stage myths and mysteries about the nature of reality would become more refined, sometimes questioned.

Gradually, humanity would become less religious and more secular. Humans would begin to be bold and invent different ways of coping with the world. The third stage saw humans moving into the stage of scientific thought. The supernatural, illusions and myths would disappear as education and rationalism spread. Humans would use observation, perceptions and rational evidence to unravel phenomena. There would be determination to move from religious and mythical interpretations to realistic and factual evidence. Rational thought and empirical evidence would run and rule the social world.

4. Karl Marx (1818- 1883)

Karl Marx was born in Germany in 1818. Marx studied philosophy at Berlin University, and later edited a radical paper. In it he criticized privileged groups who hindered progress and development. That brought him into conflict with the authorities who made him flee to England. There he lived a life of poverty. Most of his children died from lack of food and medicine. He had first hand personal experience of the whip of hunger and grinding poverty. Together with Fredrick Engels they organized the first International Workingman's Association.

Founder of Conflict Theory

He was the founder of Marxian socialism and conflict theory. He argued that the competition of individuals and groups for wealth and power is the fundamental process shaping social structure. He postulated that social structure could be put into two major categories of infrastructure and superstructure. Infrastructure would constitute material and physical things like land, buildings, physical structures. These together with raw materials, minerals, commerce and industry would constitute the means of production. Along side the means of production would be forces of production such as factories, machinery, equipment, technology, expertise and markets. The infrastructure would be serviced by the superstructure such as economy, politics, ideology, religion, education, mass-media. Who ever controlled the means and forces of production would inevitably control the superstructure, and eventually the world. Out of this analysis came Marx's theory of political economy.

Emergence of Classes

Society would evolve through critical stages of development. He called these stages epochs. These would range from primitive communalism, feudalism, capitalism, socialism and ultimately communism. So because of different vested interests between those who control the means, forces of production, the infrastructure and superstructure classes would emerge. Those who controlled, and owned, the infrastructure and superstructure would constitute the capitalists, the upper class, the ruling class. These would be followed by captains of commerce and industry, who became the bourgeoisie, then the petit bourgeoisie, that is the middle class. The next class would be the low class constituting the working class. He called this class the proletariat. Because of these classes, with conflict of interest, a natural struggle would ensue. The upper classes would exploit the resources, the workers and peasants to the upper class's advantage. Surplus value of products would lead to disparities in income, profit and interest. The predatory nature of capitalism would lead to exploitation and extreme inequality.

The Rise of Social Dynamics

All this would set in motion social dynamics. A class struggle for the ownership and control of the infrastructure and superstructure would result in overt as well as covert manoeuvres in the ideological, political, economic and social arenas. The ruling class would attempt to keep the revolution in check through persuasion, subterfuge, wage slavery, the whip of hunger. They would use the ideological apparatus such as religion, the mass-media, education and politics to cow the social revolution. They would sponsor the proliferation of religious churches to divert attention from the gross economic disparities. To Marx religion is the sigh of the oppressed creature, the sentiment of a heartless world, the soul of soulless conditions…Indeed the opium of the people!

For Marx, social history is the history of class struggle. His theory of materialism postulates that all that is solid melts into air. So, human ideas change with changes in the conditions of their material existence. Of the proletariat revolution he called on the workers of the world to unite, and rise! For they had nothing to lose save their chains of slavery!

Inevitable Overthrow of Privileged Classes

Marx believed that over the long run, the class struggle would lead to the overthrow of the rule of the privileged classes. This would result in the abolition of private ownership of the means and forces of production. To Marx, the progression from capitalism, to socialism and eventually communism was inevitable. So Marx's conflict theory stressed the importance of class, stratification, inequality, conflict, and material interests.

Capitalist Adaptability to Change

It is critical to make a comment on the Marxian conflict theory. This is an extension to Marx's analysis of power and influence. Marx did not perceive the adaptability of capitalism to changing and prevailing situations. Faced with stiff and persistent opposition from the proletariat revolution, capitalists accommodated the workers' demands for equality by bringing in the welfare system. In it, they provided elementary services like pensions, health services, insurance, subsidized education programmes, recreational and sporting facilities.

The capitalists have extended their hold on political economy. They formed mega multinational organizations that control the world's vital resources and their markets. These global organizations and companies have powerful socio economic and political tentacles. Some people call them global octopuses with total grip on the world economy. These cartels go beyond the invisible hand of capitalism that controls and rocks the global political economy.

Capitalist Sponsorship of a Super Class on World Stage

Through their superstructure, capitalists brought on world stage a new class, a super class of world elites and global personalities. Using its socio-economic muscle and control of mass social-media capitalism has created a super class that glamorizes celebrity, charisma, success, fame and wealth. The working class has been compromised since it has seen people from humble beginnings rise to super stardom through sponsorship, luck, ability and hard work. These personalities range from sports persons, actors, musicians, rich individuals, celebrities, presidents and outstanding clergy.

These individuals of fame wield a lot of power, influence on opinion and character. They can shape people's, and global, destiny, positively or negatively, depending on place, time, situation, era, point of view. They make, and endorse, presidents, policy, world views, norms, mores and values.

5. Durkheim Emile (1858-1916)

Durkheim belonged to the French school of sociology. He saw society as an organic structure with a number of essential functions. Like an organism society had essential organs for it to function well. If one of the organs malfunctioned it would result in dysfunction. So, for society to function properly, there should be organic solidarity. Durkheim sought to establish sociology as a quantitative, academic science. The model for the scientific analysis of social rates had to be explained causally. Social facts, such as suicides, divorce and crime, should be explained by other social facts.

A Normative System

His functionalist theory was the opposite of the conflict theory in that he emphasized social integration, structural differentiation, and a normative system with harmony at its core. Durkheim saw the division of labour in society as a cooperative, functional specialization, regulated by the normative system. On the other hand Marx saw the division of labour as competition of individuals and interest groups.

His analysis of social phenomena such as suicide, crime, religion, education and the professions established the functionalist sociological theory. He underlined the significance of norms, mores, values, functionalist systems and solidarity groups. So he is recognized as a sociological classic figure

6. Weber, Max (1864-1920)

Max Weber was a professor of sociology at Heidelberg in Germany. His personal life was full of contradictions. He is the founder of organization theory.

The Emergence of Bureaucracy

Though Weber agreed with Marx that economic power and rewards were major forces in societal stratification, he attempted to consolidate analyses of both ideal and material motives in human social behaviour. He saw society moving progressively from traditional structures to modern bureaucratic structures. This was the result of the modern development of rationality through studies like science, ethics, law, mathematics and general education. But he saw bureaucratic structures and social organizations leading to an iron cage. This phenomenon would lead to social disenchantment of the world, the restriction of human spontaneity, and the erosion of human values. (Popenoe, 1993). However, rationalization would set in to resolve conflict. All this would lead to the development of rational capitalism, rational bureaucracy and rational state. Like water, all these would find their level.

Weber on Classes

On classes, Weber postulated that this depended on a person's position in the market economic system. This determined one's market situation. To Weber, a person's class situation is basically their market situation. Weber identified three dimensions that would stratify people. These were the economy, politics and social status. (O'Donell, 1996). So, conflict was likely to increase when the 3 dimensions were closely related with movement being limited between strata. Although wealth, power and status tended to go together they did not necessarily overlap. People who normally work for the marginalized accrue social status but not wealth and power. Examples are Mother Theresa, Mahat MaGhandi, Nelson Mandela. Weber saw a diversification of social classes through an expansion of rational bureaucratic administration. He saw diversification of social classes rather than polarization.

Weber on Administration, Management and Bureaucracy

Generally the term administration is used for public organization such as government ministries, local government, schools, and health facilities where the main function is to implement given policy. The power and personal organizational structures predominate. The control of the organization is held by a small group of individuals who coordinate most of its activities. People in the organization are rewarded or punished through a system of patronage.

On the other hand, the term management refers to the organization of enterprises where formulation of policy, planning of goals, aims and objectives are expected to come from officials and staff. Management functions are found in industrial, commercial, business enterprises where initiative and creativity are highly valued, and actively encouraged. This system is characterized by task organizational structures. A task culture is developed aimed at achieving planned, well stated goals, aims and objectives. Team work, success and achievement of goals are underlined by a series of incentives.

The bureaucratic organizational structure involves people in the organization being given specific and well defined roles and tasks. There is a clear hierarchy with well defined rules, regulations and status. Roles and positions are prescribed. Work is divided according to sections and departments with heads of department coordinating the tasks to be done through a centralized leadership. Final accountability lies with the centralized leadership.

On bureaucracy, Weber said that it came out of the modern technological, industrial and commercial enterprises that needed a systematic and orderly form of social organization. He noted that there were small and large bureaucratic organizations. He said the term applied to all forms of organizations whether in the public or private sectors.

He had 5 bureaucratic characteristics. The first characteristic is that there is a chain of command and authority, from the highest to the lowest. Members of the organization carry out their own special tasks. Promotion and mobility depend on seniority, experience and proficiency. It should not depend on personal relationships. The organization depends on files, records, memos' precedents and so on. No individual initiative is allowed outside protocol and social practice. The last, but very important characteristic, is that members of the organization have to follow and obey a system of rules and regulations, usually set in formal binding document.

In theory and practice, persons should be appointed on merit, qualifications, experience and suitability to the post applied for. But in Africa in general there is no sharp separation between public and private life as the bureaucratic system entails. There is an irrational tendency to prefer a relative, college mate, friend, fellow tribes person, fellow villager over a more qualified and suitable candidate for a job. It is not what you know, but who you know, to land a job.

The Interpretive Theory of Religion

Weber, besides developing a theory of bureaucracy, consolidated the interpretive theory of religion in his volumes on Judaism, Christianity, the Protestant Ethic, Confucianism, Hinduism and Islam. In his theory of religion he compared and contrasted the different methodologies of harmony with people and nature, the work and profit motive, the missionary zeal and the retaliatory justice of different religions.

In the Protestant Ethic and the Rise of Capitalism (1904) Weber argued that the origins of capitalism were to be found in the changes in ideas and attitudes that spread through out much of Western Europe five centuries ago. A radical new attitude developed towards creating wealth utilizing new and powerful technologies. Weber observed that Christianity at that time became obsessed with the problems of the earthly world, and less with the problems of the spiritual world. The way to salvation became less dependent upon prayer and purity than it was upon what one did with one's life on earth. Hard work, self-discipline, modest living and saving for the future generation were the sure way to salvation. (Bloom and Ottong, 1987).

Human effort for success was celebrated in the saying that one should not wait for the iron to be hot before striking it, but to make it hot by striking! Because of the protestant ethic an unprecedented burst of productive energy swept Europe. Building, producing and constructing using the new technologies changed the face of Europe. All this led to urban and industrial employment, improvement in wages and savings.

The Need for Colonies

The need for raw materials, markets and influence meant there was need for colonies in Africa and the new world. The sequence of events smelt of the Protestant Ethic: First came the explorer, usually explorer cum missionary, then the missionary with Bible in hand, then the hunter with gun and prospecting kit, then the anthropologist eager to learn the socio culture of the people … last but important the occupier with compass, map and boundaries. Where there was resistance to occupation the fire power of military might sealed the fate of the indigenous people. The indigenous people would provide the cheap labour, most of it on a forced labour basis. The Bible talked of the hewers of wood and the drawers of water…and espoused the virtues of the poor inheriting the kingdom of heaven.

But for the colonies and post colonial states, little change took place for the average, ordinary person. Few countries have become capitalistic economies. Most countries are a mixture of peasant agricultural communities with a small sector of urban industrial activity. This has resulted in many of the socio-economic norms, values and political systems of the rural agricultural way of life persisting. This has prevented the emergence of the ways of life, attitudes and values more suited to an urban industrial and commercial society.

West's Preoccupation with Profit, Savings and Investment

It is useful at this point to return to Weber's observations regarding the West's preoccupation with profit, savings and investment. Countries with more successful economies also have proactive attitudes and values towards saving and investment. In Africa the tendency is to spend all incomes on consumption rather than investing for the future. Preferences go for consumer items than on durables. Flashy cars, suits, luxury food and items take precedence over investment portfolios. This is very common among individuals, corporate and public figures. Julius Nyerere once called this practice progress without development signified by a flashy Mecerdes Benz car parked next to a grass thatched hut! If we add to this, belief systems like witchcraft, magic, myths and superstition the barriers to development become insurmountable.

Weberian Tools of Analysis on Africa's Problems of Development

So Africa would continue to provide raw materials, cheap labour, and markets for the West's finished products. In any case most of Africa's current problems, such as food shortages, lawlessness, corruption, tribalism and the instability of government could be better understood if we use Weberian analysis. For Weber would argue that however naturally endowed with natural resources the country is, there is no socio-economic development unless the people have the organizational skills, right attitudes and values towards investment for the future.

Weber on Power, Authority and Legitimization

It is also pertinent to use Weber's analysis to examine his ideas on power, authority and legitimization. Weber defined power as the probability that an individual or group would be obeyed. Power could be positive or negative. In other words power is the effective capability of individuals or groups to make and enforce their will and decisions on matters that affect others. Authority is the socially acceptable justification for power (Bloom and Ottong, 1987). There are many ways in which power and authority are legitimated in society. Popular vote is the most common method of legitimating power and authority. People invest their faith in individuals to carry out policies on their behalf. However, this is borrowed power which can be withdrawn by the people as they wish. There are other traditional ways of gaining power and authority. Examples are claims to power and authority from supernatural forces, personal charisma, charm, subterfuge, even sheer force.

The Uncertainty and Transient Nature of Power and Authority

However, Weber was struck by the uncertainty and transient nature of power. He observed that today's powerful are tomorrow's powerless exiles or prisoners. Today's president could be tomorrow's prisoner. Those who obey today could change their minds and resist tomorrow. The government's authority could be challenged if people realized that the government has failed to deliver on promises and expectations. When that happened the government would have lost both authority and legitimacy. The normal route is for that particular government to resign or call for elections. Democratic governance rests on the principle that people should freely participate in choosing who should govern them. There can be no lasting peace and security unless there is a good measure of consent from the people. There should be agreement about the social system. For Weber this principle is applied to all forms of social organizations be it the state, church, school, college, university, or family. Authority in a democratic system is checked and tested by free and fair elections.

Sins of Commission and Omission

But authoritarian governments believe in unqualified power and authority. The ruling group feels it has the divine right to run, and even ruin, the country. The motive for staying in power lies in sins of commission and omission. So they try to remain in power by subterfuge, coercion, fear and brute force. In much of contemporary Africa, power has been openly coercive, maintained by force or threat of force. Niccolo Machiavelli's dictum becomes the doctrine. The rulers believe that they have the right and duty to seize, and maintain power by any means. They alone have the moral right to rule for ever. They employ spin doctors to manipulate and distort truth and facts to suit their masters' dictates, feelings and sentiments. Law enforcement agencies like police, judiciary, prison services are compromised. Injustice, selective justice, basic human rights violations become the norm. . When this happens the government would have lost real power, authority and legitimacy. It would be a matter of time before the people reclaim their power, authority and freedom. This is the spring of revolutions.

7. Spencer, Herbert (1820-1903)

Herbert Spencer is an early British sociologist and the protagonist for social Darwinism. He propounded the social Darwinism theory of the survival of the fittest. He argued that society progressed on the basis of individualism, biological fitness. Biological and hereditary forces influenced human behaviour, success or failure and so on. The acquisition of material things, property and the emergence of classes were part of human biological nature. This theory was in conflict with the social and environmental one that emphasized influences on individuals and groups. So insights that human behaviour was socially shaped by culture, family, class, religion, gender, education were fallacious

From 1890 to 1920 English social theory was driven by Darwinism. Laissez faire, winner takes it all and strong-manship tactics were considered acceptable. These values could have driven the expansionism and imperialism of the time. The age of enlightenment and its socio-environmental push has eclipsed Spencer's social theory.

Motives Deriving from Darwinism

But even today conservative groups' calls for individual effort, work-ethics, enterprising people, derive their motives from social Darwinism theory. Complaints relating to the welfare socialist state, group-work, donor driven programmes and aid packages to the disadvantaged echo Spencerian sentiments. The practices of dictatorship, genocide, violence and intolerance emanate from social Darwinist theory. Most brutal actions by dictators seem to confirm Socrates' statement that autocrats are not born but excreted. But it is also interesting to observe that the weak can turn the tables against the fittest. The indomitable spirit of resistance, the human desire for liberation and freedom inevitably spring up to remove the dictatorships. But the fittest, just like the dictators never learn from social history. Instead they always want to teach social history a lesson…until it is too late!

8. Mead, George Herbert (1863-1931)

George Herbert Mead taught at Chicago University School of Sociology, in the USA. He is regarded as the founding theorist of symbolic interaction. He believed that human actions were governed by the meanings that actors gave to their actions and situations. As people interacted meanings were established. He used the framework to analyze individual and group socialization patterns in society and education. These were further extended to the study and analysis of gangs, classes, racial and ethnic groups in Chicago.

Symbolic Interaction

Mead was primarily a philosopher who believed that young children develop as social beings by imitating the actions of those around them. In the process of using symbols and role playing they develop meaning and sense of self. Symbolic interaction stressed that there are different view points and ways of looking at the world. These constituted definitions of the situation. So human action cannot be objective, or predicted. Identity theories such as multiculturalism, feminism, Afro-centric theory, Queer Theory, Third worldism are very close to symbolic interaction.

9. Mills, C. Wright (1916-1962)

Mills is regarded as the founder of modern conflict theory. Although he taught sociology for 12 years he was a prolific writer. He died at the comparatively young age of 45. But his influence on American sociological thought was immense. His theory centred on two important concepts, the power of the elite, and the sociological imagination. He argued that the task of the sociologist was to see social structures and personal actions in their interrelations. Social structures were a result of struggles and negotiations between people with different interests and different resources. So, conflict would be shaped by the social structures and by the unequal distribution of power and resources in society.

The Sociological Imagination

Mills said that the sociological imagination enables its possessor to understand the larger socio historical scene in terms of its meaning for the inner life and the external career of a variety of individuals. The first fruit of this imagination, and the first lesson of the social science that embodies it, is the idea that the individual can understand his own experience and gauge his own fate only by locating himself within his period… The sociological imagination enables us to grasp social history and biography and the relations between the two within history. That is its task and its promise. To recognize this task, and this promise, is the mark of a classic social analyst.

The Power of the Elite

In the Power of the Elite (1956) Mills states that at the upper levels of American society, a powerful elite, had emerged from the fusion of the military elite, the corporate elite, the Pentagon, and the executive branch of government. The interests of these elites were often opposed to those of the general public, the mass of the population. So their policies were headed towards increased escalation of conflict, production of weapons of mass destruction, and quite possibly the annihilation of the human race. This scenario is replicated in super powers of Europe, Russia and China. The powerful elite rock, and control the social world, so it seemed. This socio political world has been dramatized by social commentators like George Orwell's 1984, and Zbigniew Brzezinski's technotronic era. The era has been characterised by 'shock and awe' doctrine of autocratic regimes that systematically worked on the gradual appearance of a more controlled society. Such a society would be dominated by an elite, unrestrained by traditional norms and values. Eventually it would be possible to assert almost continuous surveillance over every citizen, and maintain up to date complete files containing even the most personal information about the citizen. All this has been justified under state security. But the real issue is, of course, not state security, but state authority and power. The idea is to create a compliant world population controlled by state centric system, with unearned power and privileges conferred by that system.

The system works hard to protect its elite positions against the vast impoverished majority. The majority would be deprived of socio economic, geo political power and personal privacy and freedom. The other compelling reasons for individual surveillance are located in the failed, or, failing governance of the developing world. These states spawn social uprisings, instability and terrorism, both local and international.

The other reason for the system's fear lies in the moves for emancipation campaigns of the social media using the internet. The perceived threat to state centric systems comes from information freely available on the internet, and successfully exploited by non state actors who expose state excesses, corruption and official graft. Geo political analysts believe that a global awakening through social media on the internet threatens the world of the social elite. All this has created big problems for the powerful elite, the world order and the state centric systems, even more than the threat of armed insurrection. The fundamental question is: Can the underclass claim individual sovereignty and personal freedom through whistle blowers on the internet?

Enter Communications Hacking and Spying into the Power of the Elite

It is interesting to note the emergence of new communications networks that are making critical inroads into what has been a secret world of the powerful elite.

A classic example is WikiLeaks. It is an international non profit organization that publishes submissions of private, secret, and classified media from anonymous news sources, news leaks, and whistleblowers. Its website was launched in 2006 under the Sunshine Press organization. WikiLeaks' founders are a mix of dissidents, journalists, mathematicians, and start up company technologists from Australia, China, Europe, Taiwan, South Africa and USA. Julian Assange, an Australian computer programmer, is generally described as its director. The website was originally launched as a user editable wiki (hence its name), but has moved towards a more traditional publication model and no longer accepts either user comments or edits. Its main tool of access to cables is a file decryption key (similar to a pass word) to produce an encrypted version of materials stored in cable archives, official and private. It claimed data base of 1.2 million documents within a year of its launch.

WikiLeaks obtains most of its secret information from the servers of Stratfor, a US based global intelligence gathering firm, with about 300 000 subscribers. Stratfor provides confidential intelligence services to large corporations and government agencies such as the US department of Homeland Security, US Marines, and the US Defense Intelligence Agency. WikiLeaks, the classified document hacking and leaking organization, to strengthen its power base, has partnered with 25 media organizations around the world such as European and American newspapers. Another secret spilling organization called Anonymous, hacked Stratfor's web of informers, pay off structure, payment laundering techniques and socio psychological methods. This is proof that no system, no matter powerful, is safe from being exposed.

WikiLeaks Cables has revealed highly secretive conversations on sensitive issues by senior government and military officials in the world. .It has been able to spy into cables communication between high placed authorities gossiping about highly secretive information only recently privy to the powerful elite of the world. The website has gained popularity by leaking the United States of America's diplomatic cables containing information sent from US embassies around the world. WikiLeaks also lifted the lid on the extrajudicial killings in Kenya. It also exposed the dumping of highly toxic waste on the coast of Ivory Coast. It has become the world's most read whistleblower raising levels of mistrust and suspicion among senior political, social and economic players of the world. Assange claims that his WikiLeaks website has more classified documents than the rest of the world press combined.

In 2013 Edward Snowden released articles based on materials leaked from American National Security Agency. The Snowden revelations detailed the extraordinary reach of the invasion of individual freedom and privacy under the guise of national and global security. The power of the elite is being neutralized by non state actors like Edward Snowden, Bradley Manning, and by implication, Julian Assange.

It cannot be ruled out that more whistle blower websites can appear on the scene to challenge the hitherto secret world of the powerful global elite, without fear of legal or criminal charges.

10. Wilson, William Julius (1947- active)

William Julius Wilson is an eminent African-American sociologist who rose to prominence through his contemporary conflict theory. In 1997 he was elected President of the American Sociological Association. His focus is on the continuation of racial inequality mainly because the structures of racial privilege and racial inequality have not changed, though the set of legal restrictions of direct personal discrimination have gone.

The Social Structure Remains in Society

He further argues that central in today's America, are the social structures of jobs, personal networks, and residences, leading to social isolation and lack of access to employment. In other words, racism and racial inequality should be understood in terms of the larger structures of class and power in the United States.

He has written a number of books such as Power, Racism and Privilege, The Declining Significance of Race, When Work Disappears and The Truly Disadvantaged. The running themes are that loss of jobs and incomes drive underclass formations. The jobs seem to disappear from the underclass, which is mainly black, yet whites continue to have most of the 'disappeared jobs'.

The Emergence of the Under Class

Wilson's analysis of the emergence of an under class has relevance to Africa where the ruling elite have joined the socio-economic status of the mainly privileged white and brown peoples. As jobs shrink and disappear most Africans find themselves on the fringe of social life. They are either unemployed or underemployed with meager incomes. The under class live in squalid conditions in residential areas segregated as townships. There are poor facilities such as sanitation, health, education and social amenities. Good paying jobs are reserved for those with political and socio economic connections. Those in powerful positions have ghost workers on the payroll whilst the poor and underclass have no jobs.

Yet at election time the underclass are cajoled to vote with promises of a better tomorrow that never comes. Meanwhile the social elite shop at Harrods of London, get treated in overseas medical facilities, wine and dine in luxury hotels; their children go to expensive, exclusive elite schools: All paid for from tax payers' money. They plunder the resources through graft, predatory corruption, arranged fixed contracts and illicit dealings in contraband. In place of entrepreneurs Africa has now tender-preneurs. So the powerful and socially connected have joined the gravy train. The colonial inequalities have continued and the socio economic gap has widened and deepened.

11. Habermas, Jurgen (1929-active)

Jurgen Habermas is a prolific writer with a rich tradition of critical theory. His associates were the group of German theorists: Adorno, Horkheimer and Marcuse. He has written 30 books. Many of the books concentrate on the philosophical issues of post modernism. His theoretical framework straddles neo functionalism, neo Marxism and Communications ethics.

The Emergence of a Post Modernist Era

Habermas defends the emergence of a post modernist era. He argues that it is possible and desirable to specify the characteristics of a rational and just society. He believes there is a real movement in that direction. In other words he embraces the basic project of the enlightenment. He is Kantian in his belief in reason, ethics, and moral philosophy (Robinson, 2002).

The Elaborate Theoretical Apparatus

Habermas' contribution to communication theory is the elaborate theoretical apparatus. In it he addresses crucial themes such as the concept of rationality of actions, social order, quest for truth and need for an appropriate theory of action. He further argues that there should be a clear distinction between public and private life worlds. A balance should be reached between mediated norms and values and the socially defined ends and meanings which constitute the fabric of the life world. .

Utilizing Herbamus' concepts of communicative action tempered by moral consciousness, and discourse ethics as tools of analysis on African nation states, it is disappointing to see the opposite happening. The truth is not told but manipulated to suit the ruling authorities. The social media are state controlled and public opinion is manipulated to fit the status quo. Editors are state appointed with most of the print, sound and picture media toeing the official line. To get the truth about events and news in, and outside, the country one has to tune in to foreign stations.

The Ideal Speech Situation

In the ideal speech situation, Habermas contends that it is possible to reflect and arrive at the truth. In that discourse one should be able to reach the merits of all social positions without coercion or manipulation. In practice Herbamas concedes that the ideal speech situation can be manipulated to suit people with different interests. So it is possible for dictators, privileged groups and special interest groups to fool at least some of the people at least some of the time.

But it is still possible, and useful, to think and aim for the truth, the good and the beautiful.   So, Herbamas carries the hope, the wish and the desire to have a social world of peace, fairness, justice and equality. The social media play a critical role in arriving at such a world life. He thinks it can be done, it can happen, given new perspectives, good will and commonsense.

12. DuBois, William Edward Burghart (1868-1963)

DuBoi was one of the rare people to straddle many areas of specialization, a paragon of intellectual excellence. He was one of those rare persons who leave an indelible stamp on the history of their time. He was a gifted orator, a great teacher, a sociologist, philosopher, historian, economist, novelist, poet, journalist, civil rights leader and classics scholar… all rolled into one person. From 1894 to 1896 he was Professor of Greek and Latin at Wilberforce University in the United States of America. In 1896 he earned a PHD degree from Harvard University. From 1933 to 1944 he was Chairman, Department of Sociology at Atlanta University, in the United States of América.

DuBoi was a visionary, peace maker and father of Pan-Africanism. In 1919, he co- founded the Pan-African Movement and was the prime organizer of subsequent Pan-African congresses; in 1919 (Paris), 1923 (London), 1927 (New York) and 1945 (Manchester). In 1961 to 1963, at the invitation of President Kwame Nkrumah of Ghana, he took up residence in Accra as Director of Encyclopedia Africana Project. The main objective of the project was to study and research into the social, political, cultural, historical and technological developments in Africa, with the view to publishing them. Although DuBoi did not live to see this project come to fruition, the idea lives on. The first volume of the encyclopedia in the form of a Dictionary of African Biography was published in 1981. We owe to him the revelation of the wealth and beauty of the African heritage, of its historical impact on Asia, Europe and the Americas, and its infinite promise for the future, a promise that springs from its glorious vitality. Mutubuki (2003) echoes this heritage to the world in Africa's contribution to world civilization through science, mathematics, philosophy, alphabet, literature and inventions. Egypt gave birth to world religions like Judaism and Islam. Through Egypt western thought in Greek and Roman civilizations grew. This vision, and dream, is summed up in one of DuBoi's poems:

> *'Here at last I look back on my dream, I sense that Africa had come, not up from hell, but from the sum of heaven's glory!'*

On 27 August, 1963, he died, as a citizen of Africa, was given a state funeral and buried in Ghana. This was a monumental tribute to a great fighter of equality, peace and freedom for Africa, America and the world.

DuBoi believed strongly in social justice, removal of racism, in racial harmony and the emancipation of the oppressed. He lamented colonialism and neo colonialism. He said that for too long have we been fed with histories which glorify the colonialist and racist politicians. They extol the exploits of their generals' brinkmanship, their buccaneers and the robber barons, as the main actors in the affairs of humanity. They choose to ignore the real moving forces of the history of the present century; the leaders in the just struggle to emancipate the great majority of the people of the world from slavery, humiliation, exploitation and dehumanization. Examples of these ignored heroes are Mahatma Gandhi, Marcus Garvey, Kwame Nkrumah, Franz Fanon, Jose Marti, Nelson Mandela, Julius Nyerere and Chief Luthuli. The time has come to recognize that people count more than guns, and that it is the liberators who have laid the foundations for genuine international cooperation. DuBoi was a true internationalist. After many years of research, he reached a firm conviction that racial contradictions and conflicts are the consequences of other more general processes like class struggle, class contradictions and conflicts. On the basis of this he embraced the idea of social restructuring on a new just and democratic basis. It can be discerned that DuBoi was informed by the conflict perspective, and in particular, by the Marxist view of society.

DuBoi was also a philanthropist who detested greed as the basic cause of poverty and suffering. He observed that to be a poor person is hard, but to be a poor race in a land of plenty is at the very bottom of hardships. He believed that the litmus test of any society could be measured by the extent that workers could organize collectively, and participate fully in the social, economic and political decisions that affect their lives. DuBoi, (1930).

DuBoi was a consistent champion of freedom for all colonies and called for the freedom of Africa, India, Indonesia and Viet Nam. Though he believed in non violence he said it was imperative that people take up arms to liberate themselves. DuBoi asked, at the 1945 Congress, how could it be otherwise, when for centuries African peoples have been victims of violence and slavery? Yet if the western world is still determined to rule mankind by force, then Africans, as a last resort, will have to appeal to force in the effort to achieve freedom. He asserted that until Africa was free, the descendants of Africa the world over could not escape chains. So he was a revolutionary who strove to destroy the system of inequality, inequity, and establish a new world order of human equality.

For people in Southern Africa DuBoi was their man, their freedom fighter and eloquent advocate for equality. He was a hero of the oppressed people of Southern Africa. He fought relentlessly for their freedom from racism in Apartheid South Africa, Namibia and white supremacist Rhodesia. He was a prophet who saw the future as history. In 1960 he wrote that the life of a non White in Southern Africa was very cheap, as cheap as the life of a Jew in Nazi Germany. He saw the Cape of Good Hope as the Cape of Evil Omen. He lamented that some three million whites in Apartheid South Africa, South West Africa, racist Rhodesia and Mozambique were determined to rule twenty million Blacks as slaves and servants. If nothing was done to reverse the unbearable situation he foresaw the next world war beginning there.

In short, he taught the people of the world that the struggle for freedom in Africa was their struggle as well. He taught humanity how to live, how to fight for human rights, how to be principled, how to be resolute, and how to succeed. In 1947 he wrote in the World and Africa:

> *'Regardless of where we are, whether we are in Africa or in the Diaspora, we are linked by a common ideology, the ideology of anti-colonialism, anti neo-colonialism and anti-imperialism. We are linked in a positive sense by our need for social, economic and political self reliance. They call it Africa, we call it home! Let no African mind or body rest until we achieve this for the total benefit of all our people.'*

DuBoi had a vision of a world without prejudice and exploitation, a world without colonies and slavery, a world based on a common humanity. That new and just world will be created by the people who have suffered oppression. These are the people of colour who will win with the support of all decent men and women. DuBoi was above all an optimist and prophet, whose vision was based on faith in the future. In his last message to the world, he said in 1960

'As you live, believe in life. Always human beings will live and progress to greater, broader and fuller life. The only possible death is to lose belief in this truth simply because the great end comes slowly, because the time is long. We always want things to have happened yesterday.'

Glossary of Basic Concepts and Terms

Abbreviations Used in Footnotes: Common abbreviations used are ibid which is short for ib-idem, a Latin adverb, meaning in the same book, article, passage; op cit, Latin opere citato, meaning in the work already quoted or cited; loc cit, Latin locere citato, meaning in the work already located, or as indicated. So the word citation comes from Latin, the language of the Roman Empire. Because of its brevity and conciseness Latin is used in academic and professional studies such as sciences, medicine and law.

Absolute Poverty: The term is used to describe a situation where an individual, or group of persons, cannot meet basic needs like food, shelter, clothing, safe water and sanitation. This is usually used in comparison to relative poverty where people would have met the basic needs but are different in levels of comfort, wealth and luxury.

Addiction: A fixed pattern of behaviour which is difficult to change.   It may be as a result of a substance or habit such as drugs, or excessive addiction to work, cleanliness.

Administration: The term administration is used for public organization such as government ministries, local government, schools, and health facilities where the main function of officials is to implement given policy. The power and organizational structures predominate. The control of the organization is held by a small group of individuals who administer most of its activities.

Agrarian Society: A society whose means of sustenance is agriculture, that is, cropping, animal husbandry, forestry and fisheries.

Alienation: Basically a Marxian term that refers to the projection of human powers on to the supernatural world of deities. Generally it refers to the loss of control on the part of persons over the nature, and process of events and situations such as labour and its products, machinery, and technology. So human abilities, and processes, are taken over by other entities.

Amnesty International: It is an organization of ordinary people from across the world standing up for humanity and human rights. Its purpose is to protect individuals wherever justice, fairness, freedom and truth are denied. www.amnesty.org.uk.

Animism: A belief that events in the world are cotrolled and mobilized by by the activities of spirits and the supernatural world.

Anthropology: A social science that is closely linked to sociology. It concentrates on the study of traditional socio cultures, and the evolution of human species. Its main method of study is ethnographic accounts, which are detailed and systematic recordings and descriptions of observation made in the field of study.

Arms trade: The procuring and selling of weapons of war, and armaments for profit, with little regard to the consequences. It can be done at government level, or by private contractors.

Assimilation: The acceptance of a minority group by a majority population, whereby the minority group takes over the socio culture, norms, values, dress code of the dominant majority socio culture. The colonial Portuguese regimes used it, as assimilado, to absorb colonial peoples into its dominant socio culture.

Authority: The legitimate power which a person, or a group, holds over others. Power can be exerted by coercion or force. When that happens it becomes illegitimate. Hence, individuals and groups go to great lengths to legitimate their power and authority through means such as inheritance, divine anointment, elections, legal appointments.

Automation: Production processes done, monitored and controlled by machines and robots, with minimum supervision from human beings.

Avuncular groups: These are socio psychologically friendly, helpful and caring groups with similar expected behaviour, norms and values. These are also referred to as multi parenting social groups. Extended families and other kinship groups can form multiple parenting systems that share the critical tasks of rearing and bringing up children. In most parts of Africa, Asia and South America children literally belong to the village.

Biogrammar: Is a genetically based programme which predisposes humans to behave in certain ways. Though these predispositions can be modified by socio culture, they remain basic influences on human behaviour.

Bureaucracy: An organization of a hierarchical order which takes the form of a pyramid authority. Max Weber argued that bureaucracy is the most efficient type of large scale human organization.

Capital: Refers to wealth, money or assets used to invest in a business enterprise in the hope of making a profit.

Capitalism: A system of socio economic enterprise based on strictly market forces and exchanges. The motivation is making and maximizing profits. Nearly all industrialized societies are capitalist in orientation.

Capitalist: One who owns the means, forces and fruit of socio economic production. The capitalist endeavours to own land, mineral resources, raw materials, business enterprises, and markets.

Caste: A form of social stratification in which an individual's social position is fixed at birth and cannot be changed. No inter marriage, or close social association between the different members of different caste groups are permitted.

Class: It refers to socio economic difference between groups of individuals which create differences in prosperity, wealth and power.

Class conflict: Struggles for socio economic, political and ideological power between classes in society. Karl Marx believed that class conflict to be the source of divisions and antagonisms in society.

Class structure: It refers to the distribution of classes in society. Classes are mainly based on socio economic inequalities in life. Examples of classes are upper class, middle class, working class, and under class.

Codified knowledge: It refers to systematic forms of knowledge such as the jargon produced by modern science. The production, distribution and consumption of codified knowledge dominates, and shapes, the world.

Cohabitation: Two, or more, people living together in a sexual relationship of some permanence, without being married to each other.

Collective action: Action undertaken in a relatively spontaneous way by a large number of people assembled in a particular place or area to address a common concern. Collective action can give rise to demonstrations, sustained agitation for change and social springs. Examples are the Arab Spring, marches in South Africa called 'Toi Toi'.

Collective Intelligence: Abilities to work together by brilliant individuals on tasks and problems affecting their social life. These people would form think tanks that would put their minds and hands together to create, formulate and design strategies, models, artifacts, tools and machinery for collective application in their lives. The interest groups would enhance the utilization of inherent principles in matter, energy and basic machines.

Colonialism: The process whereby a nation establishes its rule, power and influence in a part of the world away from its home base.

Communism: This is the final, and desirable, stage of society as advocated by Karl Marx. He postulated that society would move through the stages of socio economic and political development communalism, feudalism, capitalism, socialism to communism. Communism is the stage when there is total equality, every one would collectively own the means, forces and fruits of production, a form of blissful utopia on earth. This stage would be the end of antagonism and conflict. Marxist Leninism, Maoist Marxism claimed to aim at communism, eventually.

Conflict: Antagonisms between individuals or groups in society. Conflict arises from socio economic interests, inequalities and perceived antagonism. Serious forms of conflict include violence, war and armed insurrection. Prolonged conflict calls for peace, truce, negotiation and agreement as forms of conflict resolution strategies.

Conformity: Human behaviour which follows the established norms, beliefs and values of a given group, or society. People are socialized to accept and follow a group's norms, beliefs and values from an early age through rewards and punishment. Conformity does not always mean the person accepts the social norms.

Consensus: General agreement over issues and ideas by members of a group, community or society. Functionalists emphasize the importance of consensus as a basis for social cohesion, solidarity and stability. This is in contrast to the Marxists who argue that it is conflict that makes the social dynamics of society.

Correlation: This is the degree to which two or more variables are mutually related. Correlations can be positive, negative or arbitrary. A positive correlation between variables exists where a high rank on one variable is associated with a high rank on the other. A negative correlation is where a high rank on one variable is associated with a low rank on the other. An arbitrary correlation is where the ranks have no relationship at all, in fact, it is zero correlation. Examples of correlation studies are race and intelligence, gender and achievement, productivity and profit, training and production, benefits and worker retention, pollution and worker health.   The correlation coefficient is a formula that is used to calculate the levels of correlation.

Correlation analysis: A statistical technique applied to determine the extent to which a relationship exists between two acts of information.

Creativity: Imaginative, innovative, original thinking or problem solving. It is the ability to think outside the box of ordinary life experiences.

Crime: Behaviour, or action that contravenes social norms of a group or society such as laws, regulations and commandments. Very few people have not broken the norms of society in one way or the other in their lives. People occupying positions of authority do commit serious crimes such as theft of public property, violence, murder, rape, and abuse of power. The International Crime Court deals with crimes of the powerful against humanity such as genocide, mass murders, mass rape, looting of national and individual resources.

Critical Thinking: Ability to use all the senses to observe relations in nature, environment and life. It is the ability to assess, evaluate and analyze situations, conclusions, by logically and systematically examining the problem, the evidence and proffer solutions.

Cult: A fragmentary socio cultural, or religious, group to which individuals, apparently dissatisfied with the existing order, are affiliated.

Cultural Reproduction: The transmission of social norms, beliefs and values from generation to generation. The term refers to the social mechanisms by which continuity by which socio cultural practice and experiences are sustained over time. The family, group, community and school are socialization mechanisms and agencies of socio cultural transmission.

Culture: The norms, values, language, beliefs, material and non material goods of a given group, community or society. Socio culture is one of the most distinctive characteristics of human social association.

Cyberspace: A world of electronic networks of communication, or interaction, between individuals at different computer terminals. They share norms, values, ideas, information and knowledge leading to the development of cyber culture. This helps to create an information society closely bound up with the rise of information technology, science and socio cultural communication

Democracy: A political system that allows its people to participate fully, and freely, in political, social and economic activities and decision making processes of the country.

Deviance: Behaviour, or actions, which do not conform to the norms, laws and values held by members of the group, or society. Deviance is a relative term, dependent on a group's norms, laws and values. However, there are universal norms and values that a person should conform to, such as those enunciated by the Biblical Ten Commandments, the United Nations.

Discrimination: The process of denying other people of resources, or rewards, they are entitled to on the basis of class, race, colour, ethnicity, gender, religion or affiliation.

Division of Labour: The division of a production system into specialized work tasks, or occupations, creating socio economic interdependence. The division of labour can be at the local, national or international levels.

Documentary research: Research based on evidence drawn from the study of documents, official records and statistics, or archives. Though authentic they may pose problems of accuracy, veracity and reliability.

Domestic Violence: Violent behaviour by a member of a household against another. Domestic violence can be carried out by males against women, adults against children, powerful members against powerless members.

Downward Mobility: Social status movement in which individuals find themselves in worse situations than before. It could be due to demotion, loss of job, unplanned retirement, illness or other misfortune.

Dysfunctions: Social influences found in groups, or society which are disruptive, or lead to the disintegration, of the normal functions of the group or society.

Economies of Scale: Economies of scale occur when companies manage to organize production on a large scale, and more efficiently. Prices of production are likely to fall leading to bulk quantities and cheaper capital.

Education: The term comes from the Latin word educare, which means to nurture, to rear, and raise carefully. So, education is the process and practice of learning and teaching skills, knowledge, norms, values and language. It is the transmission of knowledge, norms, values and so on, from one generation to the next through formal, informal and non formal means. The teacher is critical in the process and practice of education; as the ancient Egyptians would say 'the teacher clears, cleans, licks and opens the lion cub's eyes and senses!'

Egocentrism: An infantile characteristic found in children, even adults. Egocentric thinking involves understanding of objects, events, processes and circumstances in the social environment in terms of one's position, not anyone else's.

Emotional Intelligence: An acquired ability by an individual to be in tune with own emotions and the emotions of others. It involves the ability to see others' points of view, empathize and feel for others. The individual has a balanced view of the essence, and value, of the sanctity of human and animal life.

Environmental Ecology: A concern for the preservation of the integrity of fauna, flora and physical states of nature, in the face of the effects of modern industry and technology.

Estate: It is a form of social stratification involving inequalities between groups of individuals established by law.

Ethical religions: Religions which rely on the ethical appeal of a great leader or teacher such as Buddha, Confucius; rather than belief in supernatural beings.

Ethnicity: Socio cultural norms, values, language, dress and beliefs which distinguish members of a given group from others. Ethnic groups can be based on colour, race, class, socio economic status; and may lead to discrimination and prejudice.

Ethnocentrism: Viewing the ideas, views and practices of others in terms of one's own socio culture. An ethnocentric individual who fails, or is unwilling, to to judge, or look at other socio cultures in their own terms.

Ethno-methodology: The study of how people make sense of what others say and do in the course of their daily social interaction. It is concerned with the ethno-methods human beings sustain meaningful social interactions with others.

Evolution: It is the development of biological organisms through the adaptation of species to the demands of the physical environment.

Experiment: A research method in which variables can be worked on in and analysed in a controlled, and systematic, way. This can be done in an artificial situation constructed by the researcher, or in naturally occurring settings.

Extended family: It is a family group consisting of more than two generations of relatives living together, very close together, or in the same household.

Family: A group of individuals related to one another by blood ties, marriage or adoption. A family serves many purposes such as socio economic unit, procreation role, safety and security. There are many forms of the family, that is, nuclear, extended, single parent, same sex/ gay-parent, and child-headed families.

Femininity: The characteristic forms of behaviour expected of females in any given socio culture. This is linked to certain expected stereotypes.

Feminist Movement: An organized group od people concerned with promoting, and protecting, the rights, needs and interests of females in society.

Freudian Slip: Named after the psychoanalyst Sigmund Freud, and is defined as a mistake in speech that shows what the speaker is truly thinking. The more the conscious mind (pre-frontal cortex) wants to suppress the thought, the more the unconscious mind has to check to make sure one is not thinking it. Hence, the person thinks about it more. So the truth inevitably comes out. It is called in Latin, lapsus linguae, slip of the tongue.

Functionalism: A theoretical point of view, or perspective, based on the notion that social events and processes can better be explained in terms of the functions they serve people, groups and society. These functions and processes lead to solidarity, harmony, consensus and agreement on norms, values, beliefs, language and so on.

Fundamentalism: A belief in the importance of keeping to the basics of life, literal meanings of spiritual texts, social ethics and legalities. In Judaism, the fundamentalists such as the Pharisees keep a strict code of behaviour, rules and laws as strictly prescribed by the Torah in the Bible. In Islam, the Shiite believe in the practice and application of the Shariah laws in the Koran that prescribe accepted social behaviour regarding men and women. Both religions believe in retributive justice: An eye for an eye, an ear for an ear, a tooth for a tooth, an arm for an arm. If followed to their logical conclusions the world will end up with artificially disabled persons.

Gang: An informal group of individuals meeting on a regular basis to engage in common activities, which normally are deviant in nature and scope.

Gay- Parent Family: A family in which are found either lesbian partners, or male homosexuals living together as married couples. Some countries' laws especially in Africa, and the Arab world, out-law homosexuality. Other legal systems are silent on homosexuality, whilst others legalize it, as sexual orientation.

Gender: Social expectations about behaviour regarded as appropriate for each sex, either female or male. Gender refers to socially formed traits of femininity and masculinity. Gender studies have become favorite areas of research in sociology to date.

Gender socialization: This is how individuals are made to develop different gender characteristics as they grow up: To be male or female, that is the question.

Genre: A concept applied in media and language studies to refer to a distinct type of media product, or socio cultural item. Examples of different genres are comedy, soap opera, drama, news programmes, sport, recreational travel.

Globalization: The process and practice of growing inter dependence between different people, systems, institutions, regionally and internationally. The world is fast moving towards one world, one globe.

Global Village: A concept that is associated with the spread of electronic communication making the world within reach, just as a small community would be.   Television, cellular networks, internet and satellite communications, link up people almost instantaneously; making the world one.

Glossary: A list of difficult terms, with explanations. List of technical, or special, words especially those occurring in a particular text, explaining their meanings. The root meaning comes from the word gloss. To gloss is to give an explanation, comment, definition and interpretation of a term or word used in a text or book.

Heterosexuality: An orientation in sexual activity, or feelings, towards people of the opposite sex, for example between man and woman. Most people are expected by society to have this sexual orientation, which is considered essential for the continuation of the human species. Human procreation is an essential form of genetic investment.

Hidden Curriculum: Traits of behavior, and attitudes, that are learnt at school, but which are not included in the formal curriculum. The hidden curriculum conveys, subconsciously, values, ethos, accents and social climates that are typical of certain schools.

High-trust Systems: Work settings, or organizations, in which individuals are permitted a great deal of autonomy, and control over the work tasks.

Homosexuality: An orientation of sexual activities, or feelings, towards people of the same sex. Some countries' laws especially in Africa, and the Arab world, out-law homosexuality. Other legal systems are silent on homosexuality, whilst others legalize it, as sexual orientation.

House work: This is also referred to as domestic labour. Household chores concerned with day-to-day domestic work, usually carried out by women. Though taxing in effort, time and energy the work goes unpaid, and taken for granted.

Hunting and Gathering Societies: Human groups whose mode of subsistence is got from hunting animals, fishing and gathering fruits and plants. These societies tend to be viewed as backward, unsophisticated and looked down upon.

Hypothesis: An educated guess, or assumption, about a given state of affairs, situations, events, put forward as a basis for empirical testing.

Identity: The distinctive characteristics of a person's, or group, character and behaviour. Both individual and group identity are provided by social, or identity, markers such as names, totems, nationality, colour, race, dress, attire, language.

Ideology: Shared views, ideas and beliefs which serve to justify the interests of certain groups, usually dominant groups. Ideological systems serve to legitimize differential power which groups hold. Ideologies tend to to guard inequalities, discrimination, unfair access to, and distribution of, resources.

Impression Management: People in management positions may do certain things to impress who they consider important. They try to control the impressions others have of them by choosing what to conceal and what to reveal when visited.

Incarceration: The process and practice of placing individuals, or groups, within physically closed institutions such as prisons, detention centres, asylums.

Incest: Sexual relations between close blood relatives such as brothers, sisters, cousins, nieces and nephews. All human societies have incest prohibitions of one sort or another. Among certain social groups close blood relatives can marry for various reasons such as the desire to keep wealth, socio culture, prestige and power within the prescribed circle.

Industrialization: The development of manufacturing, processing and distribution of goods and services on a large and sophisticated scale. Industrialization has a tremendous influence on society and the social world. In highly industrialized nations a very small proportion of the population is involved in agriculture, yet their output produces surplus for export.

Information Poverty: This refers to the information poor who have no, or little, access to
information technology such as internet, television, computer, radio, and newspapers. Most autocratic systems make their general populace information poor so as to keep them, like mushrooms, in the dark.

Information Super High way: This refers to a vision for the future in which homes, schools, work places will be connected to a diversity of electronic communication system via cable and satellite connectivity.
hierarchy from one generation to the other. An individual from a working class family

Intra generational Mobility: This is movement up or down a social stratification hierarchy within the course of one's life, or career. An individual from the upper class, through misfortune, or own fault, moves down to the lowest level, for example, from a president to a prisoner…a prince to a pauper.

Justice: The concept of justice has to do with right, just and fair behavior, actions, processes and treatment of others regardless of race, color, gender, class, language, political affiliation, religion or origin. There are forms of justice. Administrative justice involves fair, fast, just, timeous and equal processing and application of social justice. Distributive justice involves fair, just and equal distribution of resources to inhabitants of a place, country, region or world. Retributive justice involves retribution, that is, punishment for wrong doing. In its crude form it is an eye for an eye, an ear for an ear and a limb for a limb. Restorative justice involves reparation of unfair and unjust practices and actions regarding human rights, resource allocation and distribution. It is restitution of past wrongs, harm or ill gotten wealth.

Kibbutzim: Communities established in Israel in which production is carried on co-operatively; and inequalities of wealth, income, class and exploitation are kept to a minimum. It is a form of socialism.

Kinship: A relationship which links individuals through blood ties, marriage, or adoption. Kinship relations form matrices of marriage, family and work. For less industrialized societies, kinship is of vital importance in many aspects of social life. It is not uncommon to see in Africa, a firm, school, university, ministry department staffed mainly by people with close kinship ties. When there is a funeral in one of the families, the whole institution closes for business.

Labeling theory: An approach to the study of deviance which saya that people become deviant because certain labels are attached to their actions, or behaviour by persons in authority, and with socio economic power

Latent functions: These are functional consequences which are not intended, or recognized by members of a social system in which they occur. These are the opposite of manifest functions

Lateral mobility: This refers to movement individuals from one position, or level, to the same without loss of social status.

Legitimacy: The belief, and assumption, that a particular political, social and economic order, or position, is valid and just. People in positions of power and influence go to great lengths to prove that they have legitimate authority over others.

Lesbianism: Homosexual activities, or attachment, between females

Life Course/Cycle: This refers to the different stages in an individual's life; from conception, birth, infancy, adolescence, adulthood, old age to death.

Life Expectancy: The number of years people at different stages of life course expect to live, for example infant life expectancy, adult life expectancy, old age life expectancy. The longer the life expectancy the better the quality of life the individual enjoys.

Life Histories: Studies of individuals' lives, background, experiences and circumstances. The studies can be based on documentary evidence, autobiographies, biographies and communication formats.   This helps to know people, learn from their experiences, understand causes of certain behaviors, and avoid certain actions.

Lone or One Parent Household or Family: This refers to a family, or household, in which only one parent, female or male, brings up a child.

Low Trust Systems: This is an organizational, or work, setting in which individuals are allowed little responsibility for, or control over, the work task.

Macro Segregation: Segregation and discrimination between large numbers of the members of different racial, or ethnic, groups, separated territorially. A typical example of macro segregation was the South African apartheid policy of homelands, called Bantustans.

Macro Sociology: This refers to the study of large scale social groups, organizations and institutions, or systems.

Magic: Rites, or activities, which try to influence supernatural beings, or spirits so as to achieve human aims. Magic exists in tension, or tandem, with religion. Magic tends to be more of an individual activity than a group one, practised by a sorcerer, magician or shaman.

Management: The term management refers to the organization of enterprises where formulation of policy, planning of goals, aims and objectives are expected to come from officials, staff and workers.

Manifest functions: These are functions of an aspect, or type, of social activity which are known, and obvious, to the group. Manifest functions are intended social activities by individuals involved in a given situation of social life.

Marriage: A socially approved sexual relationship between individuals, usually of the opposite sex. Married couples are socially expected to produce offspring and bring them up according to societal norms, values and expectations.

Marxism: A body of thought that derives its theses, direction and line of argument from Karl Marx's ideas. Marxists are followers of Marx as they interpret his ideas with different emphasis and inclination.

Mass media: These are forms of communication intended to reach out to the majority of the people such as newspapers, magazines, television and radio.

Materialist conception of history: The point of view developed by Karl Marx, which argued that economic and material factors have a pivotal role in determining historical events, processes and change.

Matrilineal inheritance: This refers to the inheritance of property, titles and privileges through the maternal, or female line.

Means of Production: The means with which the production of material goods is carried on in society. Means of production include productive land, buildings, raw materials, minerals, machinery, energy and water sources.

Melting Pot: This is the notion that ethnic differences can be combined to create new patterns of social behaviour drawing on diverse socio cultural sources. Metropolitan centres tend to evolve towards melting pots of socio cultures.

Mezzo Segregation: Discrimination and segregation between racial, or ethnic, groups in terms of areas, residence or neighbourhood.

Micro Segregation: Discrimination and segregation between racial, or ethnic, groups enforced in the details of daily life. Examples are separate recreational facilities, ablution blocks, waiting rooms, bus stops and railway stations.

Micro Sociology: The close systematic study of human action and behaviour in small units, or contexts of face to face interaction.

Middle Class: This refers to a socio economic class composed of those employed in white collar and lower managerial occupations.

Millenarianism: Beliefs held by members of certain religious movements, when cataclysmic changes will occur in the near future, heralding the arrival of a new epoch, a new era. They warn that woe unto those who are not prepared for it.

Minority Group, or Ethnic Minority: This refers to a minority group in society. Because of their distinct physical, or socio cultural, characteristics the y find themselves in situations of inequality within a society.

Mobilization: The process of agitating for action, and gearing up of groups for social collective action. Most of the time there are social prime movers vending collective conscience of grievances and feelings of exploitation, oppression and suffering.

Monogamy: A form of marriage in which each married partner is allowed only one spouse at any given time.

Monotheism: The word comes from mono, which means one, and theism, which means belief in a god, a super being. So monotheism is belief in a single, all mighty god.

Multimedia: It refers to a combination of different media requiring different, technologies. Visuals and audio are put on one medium such as a compact disc-read only memory, or random access memory which can be played on a computer, or television via DVD player.

Mutation: This is a process of random genetic change introducing an alteration in the characteristics of an organism. The vast majority of mutant organisms fail to survive. However, a tiny proportion of mutations produce characteristics which allow new species to flourish.

Nationalism: A set of beliefs and symbols expressing identification with a given national community. This also refers to socio political parties that espoused nation building through mobilization of ordinary people in a given nation state with demarcated boundaries. Nationalist politicians mobilized people to independence through cries of sovereignty, freedom, new constitution, name and flag.

Nation State: A situation in which a government has sovereign power within the confines of a defined territorial area. Nation states are single nations where the majority are citizens who consider themselves to be part of it.

Natural Selection: This refers to a genetic principle that organisms survive and prosper according to how well they are adapted to their environment. Those species which are less adaptive are weeded out while the better adapted species replace them.

Norms: Specific guidelines nd rules of conduct on appropriate behaviour in a given range of social contexts. A norm either prescribes a given type of behaviour, or forbids it. Norms are backed by positive or negative sanctions, that is, rewards and punishment. Examples of norms are constitution, act of parliament, laws, commandments.

Nuclear Family: A family group consisting of mother, father, or one of the parents, dependent child, or children.

Occupation: This refers to any form of paid employment in which an individual works in a regular way. There are duties, responsibilities, privileges and expectations to an occupation.

Oedipus Complex: This refers to a phase of early human psychological development, according to Sigmund Freud, in which a male child experiences intense feelings of love for the mother, together with hatred for the father. This may continue into adult life. This helps to explain male (sons) affinity for the mother, and female (daughters) affinity for the father that appear to be universal among people of the world. The term Oedipus comes from the

Greek classical mythology where a character called Oedipus, without knowing who they were, married his mother and killed his father.

Oligarchy: This refers to rule by a small minority within an organization or society. Because of unchecked power, lack of accountability and check and balances it leads to corruption, inefficiency and deviant activities.

Organization: A large group of individuals involved in a set of relations leading to the achievement of goals, aims and objectives. Organizations tend to be hierarchical, bureaucratic and formal in nature and operations.

Organized Crime: This refers to serious deviance by groups of people with the intention of committing illegal and unlawful activities. The groups could be involved in organized syndicates peddling contraband, prostitution, human trafficking and arms of war.

Pedophilia: Sexual abuse of young children by persons in authority and care. The abused children grow up traumatized, and are likely to abuse younger people in their care, in turn. It is a crime that is punishable by law.

Participant Observation: It is a research method widely used in sociology and anthropology in which the researcher takes part in the activities of a group or community being studied.

Pastoral Societies: This refers to groups or communities that derive their livelihood from animals that graze in pastures. They subsist on the rearing of domesticated livestock.

Patrilineal Society: This is a group of people who follow the male line of title, domicile, inheritance, identity marker, and belief.

Polyandry: A form of marriage in which a woman may simultaneously have two or more husbands. Examples are Polynesean and Nepalese societies where a woman can marry a hunter, trader and farmer for socio economic reasons.

Polygamy: This is a form of marriage in which a person, male or female, may have two or more spouses simultaneously. Polygyny and polyandry are forms of polygamy.

Polygyny: This refers to a form of marriage in which a man may have two or more wives at the same time.

Polytheism: This refers to belief in many gods. Examples are the Greeks and Romans who believed in many gods such as Mars, the god of war, Baccus, the god of wine, the god of speed, the god of thunder.

Popular Culture: Entertainment created for large audiences, such as popular films, , shows, music, videos, radio and T.V. programmes.

Pornography: Profane, naked, obscene, offending and sexual images that are not allowed by civilized society. It could be in the form of magazines, books, videos and pictures. It involves describing or showing sexual acts in order to cause sexual excitement. Pornography is illegal in most countries of the world.

Power: The ability of individuals, or members of groups, to achieve aims, or further their own interests through the control of others. Power is a pervasive aspect of all human relationships. Power and authority tend to go together since most conflicts in society are struggles over power between individuals or groups. The more power an individual or group have the more they are able to put their wishes and interests into practice. Absolute power does not only corrupt, it is absolutely delicious, leading to abuse of power.

Prejudice: It refers to the holding of preconceived ideas about an individual, or group, usually negative. The prejudicial ideas are resistant to change even in the face of new information.

Race: This refers to differences in human physical characteristics regarded as categorizing large numbers of individuals together. The usual discriminating identity markers are skin colour, hair, height, facial features, attire and religion.

Racism: The process and practice of attributing characteristics of superiority, or inferiority, to a population sharing certain physically inherited identity markers. Racism is a specific example of prejudice, positive or negative. People tend to focus on physical variations between people leading to pride, prejudice and discrimination found in many contexts of human societies.

Random Sampling: It is a method of selecting individuals to be included in a research study. It is an attempt to ensure that a group studied is representative of the larger population by choosing individuals to be included at random.

Rape: The threat, or use, of force to compel one individual to engage in a sexual act with another.   It is a serious criminal offence punishable by law.

Rationalization: It refers to the process by which modes of precise organization and calculation involving abstract rules and procedures increasingly come to dominate the social world.

Redemptive Movement: A social movement aiming to produce a return to a past state of affairs believed to be superior to the current one.

Reformative Movement: A social movement concerned with the implementation of a practical, but limited, programme of social change.

Regionalization: This refers to the division of social life into different regional settings or zones.

Relative Deprivation: Feelings of deprivation relative to a group with which individuals compare themselves.

Relative poverty: This refers to poverty defined by reference to the living standards of the majority in any given society.

Religion: A set of beliefs adhered to by members of a community, involving symbols regarded with awe or wonder…together with ritual practices in which members engage. Some religions involve miracles akin to magic performed by individuals in the group. Though most religions believe in a supernatural being, others believe in the ideas of a spiritual leader. Examples are Hinduism, Buddhism, Confucianism, and Shintoism. Half of the world's population do not believe in a god, or supernatural power.

Representative Sample: This refers to a means of social research which tries to match a group studied to a wider population whose qualities, properties or characteristics it matches.

Reproductive Technologies: This refers to scientific technologies which affect the natural process of human reproduction such as contraception, in vitro fertilization, cloning.

Research Methods: Refer to the diverse methods of investigation used to gather empirical, and factual, material, such as, information and data. Though one method may suffice, it is prudent to combine two in a study.

Response Cries: These are seemingly involuntary exclamations individuals make when taken by surprise, dropping something inadvertently, or expressing pleasure or anger. Such non verbal utterances provide clues to an individual's temperament.

Revolution: A process of socio political change, involving the mobilization of a mass social movement which overthrows an existing regime leading to the formation of a new regime. This is different from a coup detat, which is the seizure of political power through the use of arms by individuals who are intent on replacing the existing leadership. A coup aims at replacing personnel rather than the transformation of the socio political system. A revolution can also mean a sudden fundamental change in science, technology leading to socio economic transformation.

Riot: An outbreak of mass violence directed against persons in authority, property or both. Riots tend to be spontaneous but of short durations.

Risk Society: This refers to the emergence of a plethora of risks associated with an industrial society leading to personal and group calamities. Hence, individuals and groups have to be insured against accidents, illness, theft of property, fire and so on. Industrialization has led to mass risk through pollution, nuclear energy, weapons of mass destruction, and destruction of the ozone layer leading to global warming.

Ritual: This refers to formalized modes of behaviour in which members of a group or community regularly engage. Rituals involve irrational actions based on beliefs in a supernatural being, or failure to understand natural or social phenomena. Religion represents one of the main contexts in which rituals are practiced. Even secular groups practice rituals such as parades, flag raising ceremonies, funerals, anniversaries, birthday parties, graduation ceremonies, inauguration ceremonies.

Sacred: This concept is closely linked to ritual and religion. Sacred refers to which inspires awe or reverence among believers in a given set of religious ideas such as prayer, piety, solemnity.

Sampling: Taking a proportion of individuals, or cases from a larger population, studied as representative of that population as a whole.

Sanction: It is a mode of reward or punishment that reinforces socially expected forms of behaviour. Punishment is negative reward and positive sanction refers to reward.

Scape-goating: Blaming an individual or group for wrongs that are not of their doing. Minorities tend to be made scapegoats.

Science: The systematic study of the physical and social world. Science involves the disciplined observation, collection of empirical data combined with the construction of hypotheses, principles, theories and models which attempt to illuminate and explain the findings. One major feature of empirical study is the assumption that all scientific ideas are open to criticism, review, replication and revision by members of the scientific community.

Secondary Deviance: It is where a label becomes attached to an individual who has contravened a norm and has been punished for it. Primary deviance is the initial act of contravening a norm.

Sect: This refers to a religious movement which breaks away from the original orthodox group. Reasons for breaking away may range from differences on dogma, group dynamics to leadership variations in style.

Secularization: This is a process of decline in the influence of religion. Modern societies as they become scientific, and sophisticated, are prone to secularization. Phenomena are perceived to be open to empirical study, not due to supernatural forces.

Secularization can also refer to levels of involvement with religious organizations, rates of church attendance, the social and material influence wielded by religious groups, and the degree to which people hold religious beliefs.

Serial Monogamy: This refers to the practice where an individual contracts several marriages in succession, but not having more than one spouse at any one time.

Sex: Sex refers to anatomical differences which separate male from female humans. Sex is often contrasted with gender. Sex refers to the physical and hormonal characteristics of the human body. Gender concerns social learned forms of behaviour. In certain societies gender roles depend on situations, social variations and cultural inclinations.

Sexual Harassment: Making unwanted sexual advances by one individual towards another, in which the first individual persists even though it is made clear that the other party is resistant.

Sexuality: It generally refers to the sexual characteristics, and sexual behaviour of humans.

Shaman: It refers to a person who is believed to have special magical powers, such as a sorcerer, magician or witch doctor.

Slavery: It is a form of social stratification in which some individuals are owned by others as their property. It is the most dehumanizing and debasing act on other humans.

Social Change: It refers to alterations in social structure and systems of social groups. Social change is inherent in society and life in general. Social change brings social dynamics leading to social transformation, as well as new forms of social order.

Social Closure: This refers to the practices by which groups separate themselves off from other groups.

Social Distance: This refers to the level of spatial separation maintained when individuals interact with others whom they do not know well. The British would keep a wider social distance than Africans, Arabs and South Americans.

Social Groups: Collection of individuals interacting in systematic ways with one another. Members of a group share an awareness of common identity, needs and interests.

Social Interaction: A form of social encounter between individuals. So social interaction refers to both formal and informal situations in which people meet one another.

Socialization: This refers to the social processes through which young people develop an awareness of social norms, values, language and beliefs; and achieve a sense of self. Socialization involves all the social influences which modify behaviour and attitudes at all phases of the human life cycle. Primary socialization starts before birth up to the time the child is within the home. Secondary socialization starts when the child leaves home to go to the field, river, hills the bush and the school. Tertiary socialization takes place when a person learns adult roles such as employment, marriage and other occupations.

Socialism: This refers to a set of ideological ideas emphasizing the cooperative nature of industrial production with the intention of achieving an egalitarian social community. This is the Marxian stage before reaching the ultimate level of communism.

Social mobility: This is the movement of individuals or groups between different social positions. Vertical mobility is the movement up or down a hierarchy in a social stratification system. Lateral mobility is movement of individuals or groups from one region to another. Intra generational mobility refers to how far an individual is mobile in the course of one's own career, or life time. Inter generational mobility refers to how far the social position which a person reaches differs from that of own parents.

Social Movement: A large group of people who are involved in seeking to accomplish, or to block, a process of social change. Social movements usually exist in relations of conflict with organizations whose objectives or outlook, they oppose. When social movements succeed in gaining legitimate power and authority they transform into social organizations.

Social Position: This is the social identity an individual has in a given group or society. Social positions, also called social statuses, range from gender, family, racial, ethnic to occupational roles. Social positions can either be ascribed or achieved. Kingship, chieftainship, are examples of ascribed, inherited, positions whilst headship of a school, directorship of a company are achieved statuses.

Social Reproduction: This refers to the processes which sustain, or perpetuate, characteristics of social structures, norms and values over periods of time.

Social Role: This refers to expected behaviour of an individual occupying a particular social position. The concept of social role originates from the theatre where actors are expected to play different roles. So in every day life people are expected to play, or act different roles depending on contexts and situations.

Social Self: It is the identity conferred on an individual by the reactions of significant others. This is the basis of self consciousness in human individuals.

Social Stratification: The term comes from the latin word stratus, meaning layer. Strata means layers of people in society according to inequalities regarding resources. Social stratification refers to the existence of structured socio economic inequalities between individuals and groups in society. Class divisions are typical forms of stratification based on wide differences in terms of wealth, power, residential area, access to material and symbolic rewards.

Social Structure: These are patterns of interaction between individuals or groups. Most activities are structured and organized in a regular pattern. These are woven into the fabric of society underpinning and holding society together.

Social Transformation: It refers to processes, and dynamics, of change in social structures and systems of societies. Change, and flux, are social facts of life.

Society: The term refers to a group of people who live in a particular area, are subject to a common social system, and are aware of a common identity from other groups around them. Identity markers include language, name, ethnicity, origins, norms and values.

Sociobiology: It is an approach which explains the links between behavior of humans and animals, stressing biological principles and evolution.

Sociological Imagination: The sociological imagination is the application of imaginative thought to the asking and answering of sociological questions. It involves one in thinking one self away from the familiar routines of day to day life. One should think out of the ordinary through creative thinking.

Sociology: It is the systematic study of people in groups, with particular emphasis on interpreting and analyzing the social, economic, political, philosophical and moral worlds. Sociology has a lot in common with social history, anthropology, social psychology, economics, human geography and political science.

Sovereignty: This refers to the undisputed political rule of a nation state over a given territorial area. Globalization, information technology and world social dynamics have whittled away at the sovereignty of nation states. The world is fast becoming a global village.

Standardized Questionnaires: Questionnaires, as used in survey research, involve fixed categories, so that respondents have only a limited number of choices in giving their answers.

State: A political apparatus ruling over a demarcated territorial order, whose authority is backed by law and the ability to coerce. Examples of state institutions are government, civil service, municipalities, state utilities and service providers. The emergence of the state marks a distinctive transition in human history, since the centralization of political power involved in state formation introduces new dynamics into processes of social transformation and change.

Status: The social honour, or prestige which an individual, or group, is accorded by members of a society. Status honour or prestige may be positive or negative. Positive prestige status celebrities have distinct styles of life, and patterns of behaviour, which people follow. Negative pariah status personalities are either regarded with disdain, or treated as outcasts, by the majority of the population.

Step Families: These are families in which at least one spouse has children from a previous association living in the homestead.

Stereotypical Thinking: Thought processes involving rigid and inflexible categories.

Stigma: This is a social characteristic, or label, perceived to be demeaning and debasing.

Sub culture: Norms and values distinct from those of the majority, held by a group within a wider society. This is different from counter culture which runs across the grain of accepted norms and values of society. Deviant groups form cultures that contradict accepted norms and values of society.

Surveillance Society: A society in which individuals are regularly watched with their activities documented. The use and spread of video cameras on motor ways, in streets, sporting arenas, banking halls and shopping centres is a typical aspect of the expansion of surveillance. It is the coming of age of George Orwell's 1984 Big Brother Is Watching You.

Survey: A method of sociological research involving mainly the administration of questionnaires to a population being studied.

Symbol: An item or object used to represent, or stand for, another. Examples are a flag, logo and cross.

Symbolic Interactionism: A sociological theoretical approach which puts emphasis on the place and role of symbols and language as core elements of all human interaction.

Symbolic Power: This refers to power and authority exercised by means of symbols rather than by direct control. The mass media, television stations, satellite digital technologies, radio stations, web sites and newspapers have a great deal of symbolic power over the audiences and public opinion.

Technology: The application of scientific knowledge, empirical data and skills to production from the physical and material world. Technology involves the creation and invention of material machines and equipment, energy based instruments such as micro wave, electronic and electrical gadgetry.

Theoretical Approach: A perspective, a point of view, on social life derived from a particular theoretical tradition. Theoretical approaches supply over all traditions within which social scientists work. These perspectives influence the types of research, modes and methods of investigation. Examples of theoretical approaches are functionalism, interactionism, Marxian and Marxist views, also referred to as the conflict perspective.

Theoretical Dilemma: This refers to a basic theoretical problem that forms the focus of long standing debates in sociology. This is normally linked to theoretical questions posed by the sociologist when seeking to explain a particular range of observed social events and processes. The posing of theoretical questions is critical to attempts at understanding the nature of social life.

Theory: An attempt to identify general properties and principles which explain observed and studied social events and processes. The construction of theories forms an essential element of social science work. Theory is strongly linked to perspectives, research designs and methodology.

Time space convergence: The process where distances become shortened in time and space, as the speed of modes of transport and communication increases.

Totemism: A system of socio cultural religion which attributes divine and supernatural properties to particular type of fauna or flora. The monkey and baboon totem is attributed with special powers in rain making, among the Bantu people of Southern Africa. The fish and fish eagle totems allude to miraculous healing among the peoples of South, East Africa.

Transitional Classes: These are classes of a transient nature. A Marxian term which refers to classes belonging to a declining type of society, that lingers on in a new one. Examples are peasants or large land owners in a system that has become capitalist.

Under Class: A class of individuals situated at the bottom of the class system, usually composed of people from ethnic minority backgrounds. Africa's poor urban shanty and shack dwellers constitute the under class. They are deprived of decent shelter, food, clothing, sanitation, safe water, energy, education and health facilities.

University of the Third Age: The term third age refers to individuals living in retirement. The University of the Third Age provides study programmes for individuals in that age group.

Upper Class: A social class composed of more affluent members of society, especially those who have inherited wealth, own large prosperous businesses, or hold large scale productive land.

Values: Ideas held by people in groups about what is desirable, proper, good or bad. So values are general guidelines on acceptable behaviour. There are variations in values depending on socio culture.

Vertical Mobility: This refers to movement up or down a hierarchy of positions in a social stratification system.

Wealth: Material, monetary possessions held by individuals or groups in society. Wealth also refers to investment portfolios, assets, real estate, valuables, money and durables.

Working Class: A social class composed of persons involved in work of a general nature, or manual occupations. These people work in industry, mining, commerce and commercial agriculture. They get lower wages and socio economic benefits compared to upper and middle classes in spite of the fact that they produce most of the wealth of nations.

References

Akinpelu, J.A. (1992) *An Introduction to Philosophy of Education*. London: Macmillan

Albo, X and Anaya, Amalia (2003) *Ninos alegres, libres, expresivos: la audacia de la educacion intercultural bilingue en Bolivia (Happy, free and expressive children)*. Bolivia: UNICEF.

Alidou H. et al (2006) *Optimizing learning and education in Africa – the language factor: A stock taking research on mother tongue and bilingual education in Sub-Saharan Africa*. Paris: Association for the Development of Education in Africa.

Arends, R.I. (1994) *Learning to Teach*. New York: McGraw-Hill, Inc.

Barker, R.E.. (1995) *Philosophies of Education: An Introductory Course*. Harare: The College Press.

Benson, C (2006*) Girls, Educational equality and mother tongue based teaching*. Bangkok: UNESCO.

Bloom, L and Ottong, J. G. (1987) *Changing Africa: An Introduction to Sociology*. London: Macmillan.

Brzezinski, Z. (1990*) Between Two Ages: America's Role in the Technetronic Era*. Washington: Pergamon.

Cosin, B.R. (1972) *Education: Structure and Society*. Harmondsworth: Penguin

Crompton,R. (1993) *Class and Stratification: An Introduction To Current Debates*. Oxford: Blackwell

Dale,R. and Griffiths, C.(1986) *Youth, Unemployment and Schooling*. Milton Keynes: Open University Press

Datta, A. (1984) *Education and Society: A Sociology of African Education*. London: Macmillan

Deem, R (1980) *Women and Schooling*. London: Penguin

Demaine, J. (1988) *Contemporary Theorie in the Sociology of Education*. London: MacMillan

Dore, R. (1976) *The Diploma Disease: Education, Qualifications and Development*. London: George Allen & Unwin

Douglas, J.W.D (1964) *The Home and the School*. London: MacGibbon & Kee

Douglas, J.W.D, Ross, J.M, Simpson, H.R (1970) *Natural Symbols*. London: Barrie & Jenkins

Driver, G. *'West Indian Families: An Anthropological Perspective' in Rapoport, R.N. et.al (eds) (1982) Cape Town: Human Sciences Research Council*.

DuBoi, W.E.B. (1930) *Africa- Its Place in History*. Kansas City: Haldeman-Julius Publications.

DuBoi, W.E.B. (1945) *Color and Democracy: Colonies and Peace*. New York: Harcourt, Brace and Co.

DuBoi, W.E.B. (1947) *The World and Africa: An Inquiry into the Part which Africa Played in World History*. New York: The Viking Press.

Durkheim, E. (1947) *The Division Of Labour In Society*. New York: The Free Press

Dutcher, N. (2003) *Promise and perils of mother- tongue education.* Centre for Applied Linguistics. London.

Eysenck, H. (1971) *Race, Intelligence and Education.* London: Temple Smith

Firestone, S. (1975) *The Dialectic of Sex.* London: Paladin

Fisher, B.B., Fisher, L. 'Learning and Teaching Styles.' *The Education Digest* vol. XLIV, 8. 1979.

Gates, J. K. (2001) *Guide to the Use of Books and Libraries.* 5th ed. New York: McGraw-Hill Book Company.

Gardner, H., Hatch, T. 'Multiple Intelligences Go to School'. *Educational Researcher.* Vol. 18, 8. American Educational Research Association, 1989.

Gray, P. (2004) *Doing Research in the Real World.* London: Sage Publications

Gwirayi, P. (2010) *Sociology of Education.* Gweru: Mambo Press.

Hargreaves, D.H. (1976) *Interpersonal Relations and Education.* London: Routledge & Kegan Paul

Heugh K. *(2006) Mother tongue and bilingual education in South Africa.*

Holt, J. (1976) *How Children Fail.* Middlesex: Penguin Books

Hoyle, E. (1969) *The Role of the Teacher.* London: Routledge & Kegan Paul.

Illich, I. (1971) *Deschooling Society.* London: Penguin

Jhingran Dhir (2005) *Language disadvantage: The learning challenge in primary education.* New Delhi: APH Publishing Corporation.

Jencks, C (1975) *Inequality: A Reassessment of the Effects of the Family and Schooling in America.* Harmondsworth: Penguin

Jensen, A.R (1973) *Educational Differences.* London: Methuen

Kamin, L (1980) *Intelligence: The Battle for the Mind.* London: OUP

Klineberg, O. 'Race and IQ', *Courier,* Nov. 1971

Labov, W (1973) 'The Logic Of Non-Standard English' in Keddie, N *The Myth Of London: Penguin.*

Malone S. (2004) *Manual for developing literacy and adult education programmes in minority language communities.* Bangkok; UNESCO.

Marx, K. (1867) *De Kapital Vol.1* Harmondsworth: Penguin

Marx, K. and Engels, F. (1959) *Basic Writings on Politics and Philosophy.* New York: Doubleday.

Miller S. (2005) *Language and Education: Meeting the needs of linguistic minorities in Delhi, unpublished dissertation,* Institute of Education, University of London.

Mutubuki, E.H. (2003) Africa's Contribution to World Civilization and Education: *Anthropological Analysis' in Education Research for Sustainable Development.* Gaborone: Light Books

Mutubuki, E.H. (2004) *A Research Study on Gender Inequalities in Science and* Mathematics in Selected Secondary Schools in Zimbabwe. Fully funded by the University of Zimbabwe, 2001-2002.

Njobe, M.W. (1990) Education for Liberation. Braamfontein: Skotaville.

Nina, S. (1969) *Mao-Tse Tung on Contradiction.* London: Penguin.

Nyerere, J.K. (1967) *Education for Self Reliance.* Dar es Salaam: Uhuru Press.

Oakley, A. (1979) *The Sociology of Housework.* Oxford: Martin Robertson.

Orwell, G. (1967) *1984* New York: Harcourt BraceJovanovich.

Parsons, T. (1937) *The Structure of Social Action.* New York: McGraw-Hill

Parsons, T.and Bales, R.F. (1955) *Family, Socialization and Interaction Process.* The Free Press New York:

Pinnock H. (2006) Summarizing review by Heugh Kathleen. *Save the Children UK.*

Reimer, E. (1971) *School Is Dead.* London: MacMillan

Rempel, G.(2006) *Akhenaton, the Heretic King.*   Western New England College.

Robinson, S.(2002) *The Jurgan Habermas Project.* Michigan State University. .

Seke, A 'Gender Issues and Preferences in Botswana Classrooms,' *Tonota Journal of Education.* Vol. 3 No. 1, 1995

Skutnabb-kangas Tove (2000*) Linguistic genocide in education – or worldwide diversity and human rights?* Mahwah, New Jersey, Lawrence Erlbaum.

Stringer, R. 'Referencing Techniques,' *The Bulletin of the Associate College Centre* University of Zimbabwe. Vol.XX no.1, 1984.

The Open University (1984) Personality, Growth and Learning Units 1 and 2. *Learning Styles.* London: The Open University Press

Thomas W. and Collier, V. (2002) *A national study of school effectiveness for minority students' long-term academic achievement.* Centre for Research on Education, Diversity and Excellence. Berkeley: New York.

Toffler, A. (2003) Future Shock. London: Pan.

True, P (2006) *Historical Personalities and Issues.* Http//www.africawithin.com

United Nations Charter, United Nations, Department of Public Information, New York, NY 10017.

Weber, M. (1958) *The Protestant Ethic and the Spirit of Capitalism.* New York: Charles Scribner's Sons.

Woolfolk, A.E.(2001) *Educational Psychology.* Boston: Allyn and Bacon

http://www.wikiLeaks.org/wiki/main-page